Special Thanks
Father Joseph Patrick Breen
Judge Hal Hardin
Tony Orlando
Frankie Valli
Mitch Ryder
David Cassidy

And for my key to the future
Dan Auerbach
K-pop artist Psy

Posthumously
My mentors and lifelong friends
Bob Crewe
Saint Hal Gefsky

And to my Business Friends
Michael Dodd CPA
Attorney Stewart Levy
My lifelong councillor

This is the intriguing life story

of a quintessential

HIT MAN

There are two very different types of hitmen,

one who takes away life through murder

and

the other who awakens life

by creating the types of songs

that help us enjoy, and understand

God's greatest gift . . . love.

The Quintessential HIT MAN

L. Russell Brown
Sandy Linzer
Larry Wacholtz

Editing

Beverly Schneller

Front cover photo courtesy of Lisa Brown, aka Lisa Hayward

Photo of Tony Orlando by Travis Howard, Courtesy of Tony Orlando

Back cover photo courtesy of Larry Wacholtz, PhD.

L. Russell Brown photos courtesy of L. Russell Brown & family

All other photos and artwork licnesed through Adobe

All song lyrics written or co-written and provided by L.Russell Brown (all rights reserved).

Some cover quotes are referenced as "L. Russell Brown – Bio." Sandy Lee Watkins Songwriters Festival. Accessed July 19, 2017. http://sandyleesongfest.com/l-russell-brown-bio/.

The Quintessential HIT MAN

ISBN 978-1-948715-06-5 (pbk/Second Edition)

ISBN 978-1-948715-07-2 (ebk)

ISBN 978-1-948715-05-8 (Audio Book)

The rights of L. Russell Brown, Sandy Linzer, and Larry Wacholtz as the authors of this work are in accordance with the United States Copyright Law and Section 17 to include the six exclusive rights of ownership.

All rights reserved. No part of this book may be reprinted or reproduced or utilized in any form by any electronic, mechanical or other means now known or thereafter invented without the written permission of the publisher.

Trademarks are used only for identification and without intent to infringe.

Library of Congress Cataloguing or in Publication

© Copyright Thumbs Up Publishing 2019.

The Quintessential HIT MAN

Thumbs Up Publishing

1920 Adelicia Street
#501
Nashville, TN
    37212

615-495-5423
615-732-5736
lwacholtz@mac.com
Larry@360musicindustry.com

© Copyright Thumbs Up Publishing 2019

Contents

CHAPTER 1
    Who is This Guy   11

CHAPTER 2
    A Certain Madness   21

CHAPTER 3
    My Salvation   **37**

CHAPTER 4
    "A-WOP-BOP-A-LOO-BOP-A-WOP-BAM-BOOM!"   51

CHAPTER 5
    My First "Hit"   63

CHAPTER 6
    "The Weed"   71

CHAPTER 7
    A Leap of Faith   77

CHAPTER 8
    Attention!   87

CHAPTER 9
    PIGALLE   97
CHAPTER 10
    The Juke Box   107
CHAPTER 11
    "Stupido"   123
CHAPTER 12
    Lisa   137
CHAPTER 13
    Connecting the Dots   151
CHAPTER 14
    Tour-de-Force   163
CHAPTER 15
    Knock Three Times   181
CHAPTER 16
    Yellow Ribbon   197
CHAPTER 17
    Money Sharks   215
CHAPTER 18
    Schmoozing with
        the Legends   227

CHAPTER 19

It Took a Long Time   257

ABOUT THE AUTHORS

L. Russell Brown   271

Sandy Linzer

Larry Wacholtz PhD.

INDEX   285

Chapter 1

Who is This Guy?

I'm definitely tired of the business, it's not as much fun anymore. It's just gotten too damn big. I don't know the players anymore as "when I was one of the hottest songwriter on the planet". Clive Davis is still somewhat active and the other honchos are now either retired, dazed, or dead. Lucky me, I'm neither. I know in my heart of hearts I can still compete. I remember when Sandy Linzer was on staff at Epic Records and the powers that be told him his career was over.

He had just turned 30 and they suggested to him he was "long in the tooth." They gave him one last shot to redeem himself, to keep his job. He was given an assignment to produce one song, written by a new band they had just signed. Other producers had tried and failed to come up with a concept for the song and they were doubting the band would ever succeed.

With his job on the line, he took the group into the studio and produced a recording of the song. They hated it! He was let go. "Brandy (You're A Fine Girl)" by The Looking Glass is not only one of my personal favorite records of all time, but it's also one of the most successful records ever made. It went to number 1, sold over 2 million singles and is a classic that is still in heavy rotation on radio stations all over the world.

Sometimes I wish I could just retire like a normal human being. Be rewarded with a gold watch from a company that I worked for all my life, who appreciated my service, and wanted to say, "Thanks, Mr. Brown". So many companies now try to find a way of getting rid-of-ya', kickin' you out before your benefits kick in. I can't play the sympathy card and disappear heroically, like everybody's tragic hero, Willie Loman, in *Death of a Salesman*. Why should anyone feel sorry for me? I'm always bragging about my children, "The Ribbon", "The Rose", and "Knock Three Times". "Hey, do you know who I am? Guess what I wrote!" Ha!

The fact is I'm still in the game. It's almost 2020 and I've just finished writing over 70 new songs with Dan Auerbach of the superstar group the Black Keys. Psy's, the top Korean artist in the K-pop global music market, used one of my songs as the intro for one of his newest releases, and, it's had over 60 million hits on Facebook. However, probably my best memory in the business came from meeting Charlie Calello.

As my career started to wind down a little, I began working with people that as a kid from the housing projects in Newark, I'd never have a shot at meeting ever in my lifetime. One of them was Charlie Calello, everybody on the planet's 'go to guy' for hit song arrangements. I don't have enough paper to list all of the hits he contributed to with his genius.

He hooked me up with Nancy Sinatra. I was supervising a demo session in Hollywood for her when she asked me, "Would you like to meet my father at the Greek Theatre this week?" "I'll have the limo pick you up on the way to my house, ok?"

Nancy, her little daughter AJ, and I stepped out of the limo and along with a small group of gigantic Hollywood stars proceeded up the gravel path toward Sinatra's trailer. We entered a 10x10 room with an L-shaped sofa along the wall. I could hear the TV set playing in the next room. Frank Sinatra was in there watching a Dodgers game. Nancy introduced me to everyone in the room, including: George Burns, the Robert Wagners, Barbara Sinatra, and others.

"George Burns (1896-1996), was born Nathan Birnbaum in New York City on January 20, 1896. He got his start as a vaudeville comedian, developing an act with Gracie Allen. Burns and Allen launched a long partnership in radio, film and television. Burns outlived Allen by decades, during which time he won an Academy Award".[1]

Robert Wagner, and Natalie Wood were there:

> Wood was born on July 20, 1938, in San Francisco, California, as Natalia Nikolaevna Zakharenko . . . When she was just four years old, Natalie appeared in her first film, Happy Land, a bit

[1] George Burns. (2015). The Biography.com website. Retrieved 06:07, May 02, 2015, from http://www.biography.com/people/george-burns-9232145.

part of a crying little girl who had just dropped her ice cream cone. In 1946 Natalie tested for a role in Tomorrow Is Forever and she flunked the screen test. Natalie's mother convinced the studio heads to give her another test. She was eventually cast in Miracle on 34th Street... and many other movies including "West Side Story", "Splendor in the Grass" and "Love with the Proper Stranger".... On November 29, 1981, she was sailing on the yacht she shared with her husband Robert Wagner and their friend Christopher Walken, when she fell in the ocean while trying to board the dinghy tied up alongside the yacht and drowned.[2]

Next was Mrs. Frank Sinatra (the former Barbara Marx-who divorced Zeppo-one of the Marx Brothers-to marry Ol' Blue Eyes in 1973). Just when I thought I had seen it all Clint Eastwood walked in, sat down next to me and reached out for my hand. Clint F...king Eastwood was shaking my hand. WOW! I think about everyone knows him as a great actor and director and wouldn't you know, he eventually directed the movie *Jersey Boys*. It was about Frankie Valli and the Four Seasons, Bob Crewe, and, the people I've written songs for and worked with all my life.

---

[2] Natalie Wood, Biography, INDb, http://www.imdb.com/name/nm0000081/bio?ref_=nm_ov_bio_sm

Like every guy on the planet who had ever dreamed of spending five-seconds with the most beautiful girl in the universe, I couldn't take my eyes off of Natalie Wood. I couldn't imagine any guy not falling head over heels in love with her. I did, as I felt Nancy's eyes burning a hole in my back. If only I had been courageous enough back then, crazy enough, to slip her my phone number. Who knows, she might have been with us the night she slipped off the edge of "The Splendor" near Catalina Island?

Frank Sinatra (1915-1998), stepped out of hiding and I found out I wasn't alone. He made a bee line for Natalie and kissed her. Frank shook hands with Bob Wagner and I was in heaven as the two gods of the entertainment business embraced, Ol' Blue Eyes and George Burns. Nancy whispered in my ear, "Go, say hello to my father". I had been in the company of some of the biggest stars in the world. I had stood up to Army generals. I had conquered demons threatening my life at home. I had seen so much, but I wasn't prepared for this.

Here was 'The Man', the greatest living artist of our time. I had seen all of his movies, owned most of his records and like so many people around the world, I was in awe of the guy. Nancy encouraged me to go "talk to my father". I couldn't help think of Calello's story about the time he and Frankie Valli went to Rome. It was Frankie's dream to meet the Pope. When the processional passed them by, Calello saw the tears welling up in Frankie Valli's eyes at the sight of seeing his Eminence. Calello whispered to Frankie, "Hey Frank, I think this guy is bigger than Sinatra!" Hell, here I was, a kid from the Seth Boyden projects in New Jersey about to see for myself!

I walked over and shook his hand and said, "Bing Crosby and you have recorded my song 'Tie a Yellow Ribbon'. Before I finished, he suddenly slapped me hard across my face. "Where were you when I needed the tune, kid?" I answered, "Next time I have a song for you, I'll give it to Jilly". Jilly was a famous NYC club owner and Sinatra's pal. Sinatra was letting me know that he wanted to be the first to record "Yellow Ribbon" and that next time he'd like to see a similar song first. He looked at me with that look he gave Maggio in the film From *Here to Eternity* (when he threatened to kill him), and said, "You do that, kid".

Nancy smiled and later confided in me what I already knew. For her father to do that, he knew that like him, I was a street kid. It was a 'backhanded' compliment from the Chairman-of the-Board. The world had heard my songs and I'd sold millions of them. But when Sinatra slapped me in the face, I knew I'd arrived. He knew that I had the talent to write hits and he wanted to make sure he got to hear them first. I was now one of the few who had his respect, not only as a great songwriter, but as a wise guy kid who grew up in the streets of Newark, just like he did in Hoboken.

Both of us, against all the odds, had arrived where nobody would have ever expected either of us to be. It had taken me a lifetime, but I knew that I had finally arrived. I was at last accepted instead of rejected, beaten, and isolated as I was growing up. I was at last safe, respected, appreciated and loved for who I am and what I've been able accomplish through God's grace.

Chapter 2

A Certain Madness!

The bedroom was pitch black, and the only sound was me whining from the pain of my tooth when the door slammed open. Leaning forward was the shadow of a slim, short, angry man. "Shut the fuck up or I'll kill you, you . . . son of a bitch". I couldn't have been more than four years old when he started beating me. My dear sweet father threatened to murder me if I didn't stop wailing about a severe throbbing toothache. The look on his face was so fearful I whimpered myself to sleep, after being punched in the face and that was just the beginning.

Sadly, there was a madness going on inside the walls of our apartment at the housing project, a madness that as a little boy I didn't understand, until later. I was never safe. One day my father was backing the car out and my leg got caught in the door. I screamed for him to stop, he wouldn't, and when I looked over at him he was smiling.

That's what I grew up in, a world of fear, a prisoner in a dark world of evil. The deep scars his beatings left in my mind and on my leg pale next to the one I carry inside of me in my heart. The beatings had come often and I never knew when, why, or where they were coming from. I think about my kids and grandchildren . . . any child and the thought that a father could be so heinous, so cruel to me and my brothers and sisters is beyond my comprehension. But that's what I had to live with growing up.

In the movie, *The Family* actor Robert DeNiro reveals what it's like growing up as a kid in an abusive, fearful, and angry childhood (as depicted in Martin Scorsese's movie *Goodfellas*) as

> "There's an opening scene and there's a guy on the left with a yellow shirt on sitting on a chair that's turned around. He was a real gangster. Stone cold killer. You'd see him on Hester and Mulberry every morning, he'd have his coffee, just like he did when he was a kid. His father use[d] to beat him up, throw him out of the

house. This kid had a lot of aggression . . . and that's where that killer instinct comes out. He'd gotten so many beatings you just don't give a fuck. At twelve this kid had what's called a beef with . . . an argument with a kid from another neighborhood. And one thing led to another and next thing you know he beat him to death with a two by four. Put his hand in cold water. That's an expression that certain people use to use when you killed somebody for the first time".[3]

The Seth Boyden Housing Projects, where I lived from 1943 through 1957, were three stories high and each apartment was remarkably well kept. The federal government financed the construction of the project's red brick buildings to make affordable housing available for the underclass people of our time like my father, Abe Brown, our family and friends.

Each set of buildings had a courtyard the kids used as a play area. Center Terrace was ours, complete with basketball courts, jungle bars, and a large grassy field. On a hot summer day, all of us, parents, kids and our pets headed for the 'showers' (a large square-three-inch deep cement depression with a pole constructed in the center) that showered us squealing kids with cool wa-

[3] DVD. United States: Relativity Media, 2013.

ter.

We were poor, but we were still proud enough to keep the projects clean and safe. We took great pride in the appearance of our neighborhood and worked hard to keep it that way. The stairwells and the grounds were more of a challenge, but they were rarely littered. It was a multi-cultural neighborhood and most of us didn't understand ethnic differences. This was our 'country club'.

These buildings were nearly indestructible-unbearably hot in the summertime, but warm as toast in the winter. Radiators were installed in every room and blew out clean, steam heat: a good place for a kid to dry out his socks. It was easy to make contact with the kids upstairs and downstairs, knocking on the floors and banging on the pipes (childhood memories, that as a songwriter, looking for inspiration, I would tap into later).

Rumors were the news of the day. I remember a strange odor coming from a Polish family's apartment (they were cooking cabbage), so we would run like hell past their window, certain that they were cooking little kids inside! Another rumor came from down in the cellars. We heard the "Green Man" was lurking there; so, we needed to 'beware'! It was dark, and scary, but not dark enough to hide the thrill seeking teenage lovers who were spreading rumors (among other things) about the "Green Man" to keep us away from their 'hanky panky' parties. The Cleveland family was renowned in the projects. They had thirteen children, and as crowded as they were in their apartment, each kid still had their own pet, chickens, turtles, cats, and dogs were always coming in and out of the 'Cleveland Barn'!

The floors were made of a dark brown, mysterious, synthetic material that you couldn't cut with an axe. I know, I tried. And whether you had a two or three-bedroom apartment, no apartment had more than one bathroom, one sink, one small tub, and one toilet! I grew up believing "hurryupgoddamnit" was one word. Funny, that's the same word I use today waiting to access my computer. New Year's Day 1945, my kid brother,

Paul "Pinky" Brown arrived; now we were three. Then came my sister Suzy, and then Mickey, and then Steven and last, my late little brother Billy, who overdosed on coke. Did I have parents or rabbits? We needed more room in our den, and thankfully, later we were able to get a larger three-bedroom apartment.

"Abba Dabba Dabba" was the crazy little song my sister Annette and I sang into the wee hours of the night, hanging from the jungle bars, "Abba dabba dabba dabba dabba, dabba dabba, said the monkey to the chimp". A steel configuration of two-inch tubing, put together in three foot squares that climbed to 15 feet high at the top, these monkey bars were our special hangout, until we heard mom yell out from the window to come back down; back to the reality we had escaped for a while.

My roots run deep in New Jersey and its history. Extreme conservative New Haven Colony founders (better known as the Puritans) split with the liberal members of their founding church to purchase the land currently known as Newark from the Hackensack Indians for gunpowder, one hundred bars of lead, twenty axes, twenty coats, guns, pistols, swords, kettles, blankets, knives, beer, and ten pairs of breeches.

The first hotel opened in 1670 and in 1698 the first leather tannery opened. In the mid-1750s, Aaron Burr, who became the second Vice President of the United States, was born there. By 1837, there were 155 patent leather manufacturers in the city, producing leather then-valued at $899,200. The Ballantine Brewing plants covered 12 acres as the sixth largest brewer in the nation. The first round of Irish immigrants starting arriving in the 1800s, followed by Germans from the 1840s through the 1870s. Next came the African-Americans who swelled the population by 54% in the 1970s.[4]

There was a wise guy tone to the city, probably because some of the famous people who had grown up near there included Frank Sinatra (1915-1998), comedian Jerry Lewis (1926-2017), author Philip Roth (b. 1933),

---
4 Hartman, David. "A Walk-Through Newark". History. Colonial Founding | Thirteen/WNET. Accessed June 17, 2017. http://www.thirteen.org/newark/history.html.

and recording artist, Whitney Houston (1963-2012). Sinatra's story is an example of life as I remember it as a kid trying to survive on the streets. Sinatra was

> ... Born in Hoboken, to Italian immigrants Natalina Della (Garaventa), from Northern Italy, and Saverio Antonino Martino Sinatra, a Sicilian boxer, fireman, and bar owner. Growing up on the gritty streets of Hoboken made Sinatra determined to work hard to get ahead. Starting out as a saloon singer in musty little dives (he carried his own P.A. system), he eventually got work as a band singer, first with The Hoboken Four, then with Harry James and then Tommy Dorsey . . . his image was shaped into a street thug and punk who was saved by his first wife.[5]

Entrepreneurs associated with that part of New Jersey included Thomas Edison and John Hyatt, who developed camera film, and other types of electric devices. John Dryden formed a company that eventually became the Prudential Life Insurance Company of New Jersey. It had always been a place of corruption from the top down and crime often meant financial success. Leo P. Carlin (1908-1999) was elected mayor in 1952. The tough Irishman quickly took control of the city and didn't relinquish power until 1963. He was a popular

---
5 "Biography." IMDb. Accessed May 08, 2017. http://www.imdb.com/name/nm0000069/bio.

mayor even when being accused of corruption. But the tone of the city changed with the influx of so many different nationalities from political and financial crimes to raw violence between the mostly struggling white middle class and the entrenched minorities.

Superstar Whitney Houston's life, in some ways, sadly portrays the changes in Newark street life from the tough Italian and Irish street kids to the Newark of the mid- 1960s. That's when it really changed to a different type of violence based on drugs, unemployment, bad schools, and a kind of corruption in government that led to four days of rioting between whites and blacks with 26 dead, over 1,000 injuries, and millions in damages.

Not too far away from the projects was Hawthorne Ave, where, hidden behind a small storefront, lived the legendary bookmaker Jake Mohawk who presided over the neighborhood 'social club'. Everyone (including the paid-off local police) knew that Jake ran numbers, took bets on the ponies, and acted as a moneylender for the local hipsters, charging crazily high interest rates. My father's nickname was "The Weed", because he smoked grass (marijuana) all the time. When he declared bankruptcy, he actually put Jake Mohawk's name down as a creditor. Then he sent me (I was ten at the time) down to Jake's to give the papers to 'Big Jake' putting him on notice. He read them in disbelief and told me, "Tell your old man I got the message, and tell him if he takes my name off the papers he can forget the debt!" My father played the game well and knew that anonymity was crucial to the survival of Jake. According to Robert Rockaway (2000) in his book, *But he was good to his mother: The Life and Crimes of Jewish Gangsters*,

> Jake Mohawk Skuratosky... was one of Newark's more colorful bookmakers. Jake claimed that a bookmaker was the most honest person alive, because he had only one asset, his reputation... No matter what happened to Jake, whether arrested or money confiscated by the law, he always paid off, immediately.[6]

My father once told me he had performed certain 'fa-

---

[6] But He was Good to His Mother, The Lives and Crimes of Jewish Gangsters, by Robert Rockaway, Gefen Publishing House, Jerusalem 2000, https://books.google.com/books?id=PRl-wCAAAQBAJ&pg=PT82&lpg=PT82&dq=bookmaker+Jake+Mohawk&source=bl&ots=E_oNsGE13m&sig=I5v3qekePkQglPWAs6fCc9NSvLY&hl=en&sa=X&ei=1iE8VfWyFsa1ggSl94HY-Cw&ved=0CCEQ6AEwAQ#v=onepage&q=bookmaker%20Jake%20Mohawk&f=false.

vors' for Longy Zwillman (1899-1959), the Jewish brains of the mob (also known as the Al Capone of the New Jersey Mafia). Jake Mohawk knew it, and needless to say, his debt was forgiven. Zwillman was killed, but with a measure of respect. The boys came to him and told him he had to go. This is how one source tells of his end, "Longy didn't want to die, but they explained patiently there was no other way. They even brought along a bottle of expensive brandy to ease the elderly hoodlum's passage. When he was feeling no pain, they trussed him up so that he would not flail wildly and suffer and then they hanged him from a water pipe in the basement of his house".[7]

As you've probably figured out, behind closed doors, Abie, as my mother used to refer to my father, was a scary, violent man. I kept telling myself "If I can survive this bastard, I can survive anything". It felt like his favorite pastime was whacking me around. I still don't know what drove him to be the animal he was. I won't give him the benefit of the doubt or cut him any slack,

---
[7] Abner "Longy" Zwillman Crime Syndicate Founder and New Jersey boss. Carpe Nortem, Seize the Night. http://www.carpenoctem.tv/mobsters/abner-longy-zwillman/

based on the stories he used to tell us about the abuse he endured as a child. But he claimed it was so bad that his stepmother, Hattie, once tried to lose him in one of the large department stores in downtown Newark. Too bad she failed.

I also remember that on Frehlinghuysen Avenue, directly across the street from the projects, were the factories that went on for miles in both directions. The Pennsylvania Railroad tracks ran just behind them. The freight trains were loaded with all kinds of things to be shipped across the country. Wow, what a bonanza for a starving kid from the housing projects! My buddies and I had hundreds of bottles of Pepsi Cola buried in between the wooden ties of the railroad tracks. Whenever one of us wanted a drink, we would dig down into the coals between the wooden ties and pull out a bottle of Pepsi!

Frehlinghuysen Avenue, the wide thoroughfare that ran north and south in front of the housing projects, became Newark Avenue at the Elizabeth city line. A couple blocks more into Elizabeth were the long ramps that led into the Berry Biscuit Company, once known as Durant Motors. They manufactured cookies and candies, including my favorites, Almond Joys. Usually by the time the gang and I got there, we had already gorged ourselves on doughnuts from the doughnut factory and everything from soup to nuts from the A&P grocery store warehouse. If it wasn't nailed down, it was ours. At eleven years old, I had become an accomplished purveyor of illegally gotten goods. I knew the warehouses where ten-pound cans of ham were stored, along with watermelons by the boxcar, not to mention endless crates of fresh fruit, and countless cans of, yep, you guessed it, Pepsi. To this day, I have never failed a Pepsi/Coke challenge test.

As I look back on those years, I can understand now how getting even with my father, Abe Brown, The Weed, for the love he denied me was important to me. All through my childhood his constant beatings were getting to me. One day in school I'd had enough. I was the tough guy who was ready to lash out at any son of a bitch who gave me some bullshit. Sadly, one of my classmates, a blond girl, gave me the invitation I'd been waiting for. She was mad as hell at me for something I'd said in class so after class we decided to have it out. She tore her fingernails into the side of my face. I felt warm blood flowing down my cheeks, and without thinking, I coldcocked her with a right-hand punch. As she fell backward, I jumped on her and continued to beat her violently until some of the guys pulled me off. Now, as I look back at it, I just wish I could apologize to her. I have never forgiven myself. I had to take out my anger on someone and it's haunted me all my life that it was her.

* * * *

Like most of us, curiosity always got the best of me. So, one day, at the ripe old age of ten, I decided to see what kids my age were doing on the other side of Weequahic Park. I found myself walking in the tree-lined streets looking for a bike, anybody's bike! I remember ordering a 'dog' as I spun around on a stool at Syd's, the local hotdog joint on Chancellor Avenue, across the street from the high school. I sat alongside one of my possible victims who just might be riding one of those fancy Schwinn bikes that I loved. Maybe he left it close by and unlocked! Even back then, I believed in equal opportunity.

Nineteen fifty-one was a bad turning point in my life. It was only a matter of time before I tried my luck elsewhere. Constant hunger got me into trouble. If it wasn't nailed down I took it, ate it, and it was all was too easy. That led to satisfying other cravings for bigger things, like hot cars with the keys left in the ignition begging me to, "Take me, I'm yours". I took what I needed one too many times. Sadly, it was a 1951 Cadillac and I crashed it into a telephone pole in Hillside, which led to my arrest and incarceration.

Chapter 3

My Salvation

I was a tough kid fighting for recognition, acceptance, and love, and where did it get me? What I got was Judge Lindemann ordering me to "Stand", as he pronounced my sentence. I was eleven and not quite prepared for what was about to happen. Lindemann's words will forever ring in my ears. "Lawrence Brown, I remand you for an indeterminate period of time, to the State Home for Boys at Jamesburg". Tears filled my mother's eyes as they took me away. I felt ashamed and so bad for my mom, worse than what I felt for myself. My father just stood there staring in disbelief.

After several days in the parental home on Sussex Avenue in Newark, I was taken to Jamesburg, a sprawling complex opened in 1867, made up of large housing units surrounding a two block long rectangular field.

The mess hall was at one end, and another dreary building at the other end of the field housed the school. They locked the cell door and this tough little kid from the projects didn't feel so tough anymore.

Jamesburg was no *Boy's Town*. This was no movie and I wasn't Mickey Rooney. *Boys Town* was the 1938 movie about Father Flanagan who believed that "there's no such thing as a bad boy" instead of the cruel, harsh, and unsympathetic approach found in many juvenile delinquency centers. Spencer Tracy played Father Flanagan and child star (at the time) Mickey Rooney took the role of Whitey Marsh, a crippled bad kid whose brother wanted him to have a better life.[8]

The cottages were numbered and occupied according to age, which was designed to eliminate the bigger kids picking on the smaller ones. I was assigned to Cottage Twelve. When I first arrived, Mr. Rowe, the headmaster of our cottage, took me aside and said, "Larry, you're the only Jewish kid in Jamesburg. If anyone ever both-

---

[8] "Plot Summary." IMDb. Accessed July 11, 2017. http://www.imdb.com/title/tt0029942/plot-summary?ref_=tt_ov_pl.

ers you, come and tell me". Growing up as I had in the housing projects, I didn't understand what he was trying to say. I'd heard anti-Semitic slurs, but never from another kid. Mr. Rowe later confided in me that he was of German extraction and was sensitive to anti-Semitism. His words turned out to be sadly prophetic.

All the "inmates" were allowed to mingle with one another for a short time. I remember being on the field when a big nasty prick (the only name I'll ever remember him by) called me a little Jew Bastard. He took a piece of hot pepper broke it in half and scraped it hard down my back. It stung like fire-the pain was excruciating. I screamed and ran away. I reported the incident to Mr. Rowe who, knowing that if he reprimanded the bully there would be repercussions on me, contacted an Orthodox Jewish family living nearby.

The following Friday, they surprised me with an invitation to join them for Friday night services at their home. I was given clean clothes and a home cooked meal and, my only obligation was to participate in their Friday night services. This was my sanctuary, my new home away from home. I will always be eternally grateful to this loving family who adopted me during my terrible ordeal at Jamesburg.

All the "inmates" were assigned jobs, and mine was to clean the school's urinals and toilets daily. I found most of them unflushed and brimming with urine and feces. What was worse, the powerful smelling sanitizer Pine Sol that gagged me whenever I opened the containers or the smell of the poop and urine?

I was growing more desperate daily to get the hell out of there. But I didn't have anywhere to go and had to finish my court ordered sentence. I found my salvation on the third floor of the building that housed an old banged up upright piano! It was this piano and the music I played for an audience of one, Mr. Fitzpatrick, the head custodian at the Jamesburg school, that saved me from the horrid, foul smelling toilets. Fitzpatrick was Jamesburg's tough old school custodian and self-appointed disciplinarian, who made it clear to me that toilet duty was my duty.

Here I was, in the State Home for Boys, looking for any excuse to get out of my daily "shit" job. When I was ten years old, at Dayton Street School, I taught myself how to play the piano. I was driven to be good at it. I would go into the auditorium after school and pound on the keys for hours.

Mr. Fitzpatrick was always in the building and I found that old broken down, out of tune piano my salvation. I remember sitting down and wondering what would happen if I played it instead of cleaning the urinals. Fitzpatrick was an Irish name and I knew some Irish standards, so I took a chance. I began to play, "When Irish Eyes Are Smiling". No sign of Fitzpatrick. I finished that song and broke into the classic song, sure to bring tears to any good Irishman's eyes, "Galway Bay". Still no Mister Fitz. Then I broke into my best version of the Bing Crosby hit, "Who Threw the Overalls into Mrs. Murphy's Chowder?"

After about five more songs and right in the middle of another one, I peeked at the door and there he was. I was terrified but I kept on playing. I caught a glimpse of the tough old 'Paddy' peering into the room at me. He never said a word and I kept on playing. From that day on, as long as I was playing for Fitz, I didn't have to clean the toilets. The place began to smell like holy hell, but as long as Fitz was off my case, I was in heaven, which is where I know he is now and surely singing, "Tura Lura Lura".

As I grew into a teenager, Newark was quickly becoming a melting pot to rival any in the national breeding ground for new and exciting ideas. Dwight D. Eisenhower (1890-1969) was elected President following the Second World War and the United States was the most powerful nation on earth. It took a long time, but finally, I got to go home to my waiting, still violent father.

Until I was 14, my father was as tough on me as a deranged guard in a maximum-security prison. My mother, Caroline, who was gentle and never laid a hand on me, was as frightened of him as I was. At last, she started to understand his violence and its effects on me. She courageously began to pull him off of me while he continued mercilessly beating me.

I even remember once when I had a cast on my fractured right arm and I just couldn't shield the blows. Far too many times, I thought he was going to kill me. In the mid-1950's schools were not as pro-active as they are today in combating child abuse. When I was young, there was a greater sense of privacy about a student's home life, which means that the violence just continued and the results were harmful to families and community.

Outside of our apartment I always felt safe walking the streets of the Seth Boyden district. But if I happened to get lost in my thoughts and wander too far away finding myself alone in one of the tough neighborhoods in Newark or Elizabeth, it usually meant trouble was headed in my direction. That was all right with me, too.

I could take care of myself most of the time. But one day walking down Virginia Street in Elizabeth a local gang cornered me.

I was about to get my ass kicked when John Tully and his crew just happened to show up. None of them were my friends but they knew me and saw I was about to get whipped when Tully asked me, "Hey, Brown, these guys bothering you?" I nodded, and suddenly my 'ass' was safe and theirs was 'grass'! Tully told me to get home. I thanked him and he gave me something he didn't give to anyone too often . . . a smile. We were like a family within a family and I was lucky to be a part of it. John and his crew ended up where I could have, which was as hit men for the mob. The last I heard, one of them was selling hot dogs in the witness protection program and one of the other guys was dead. I wonder, what saved me from their fate?

Going to school wasn't any better. I loathed grammar school teachers like Mr. Shaffer, my arithmetic teacher. He would announce to the other kids in the class when they got a problem wrong, "How could you get that wrong? Even Larry Brown got it right". It still steams me about how he made me feel for serving time in Jamesburg. He didn't know anything about my home life, never asked, and never let me forget that I had served time in the state home for bad boys at Jamesburg.

My music teacher, whom I shall leave nameless out of respect for the dead, wasn't much better. One day, I stood at the piano, and impromptu, picked out a melody. I was so surprised-where did that come from? I was excited and I couldn't wait to play it for him. After I sounded it out, he slammed the piano keys cover shut and yelled at me, "What makes you think you can write music? You can't read a note of music, go back to your seat". His nasty behavior did not discourage me. In fact, he made me feel as if I'd written some pretty good notes on the piano and he just turned out to be an ugly man. He never realized how much of an influence he had on my life. I hated him so much I was determined to prove him wrong.

* * * *

Inspiration often comes from surprising sources. One day, Mr. Talbot, one of the very few black teachers at the school, heard me practicing alone on the piano in the auditorium. He stood silently in the back of the room and watched as I ran my fingers up and down the keys like a wild man. When I finished my song, he applauded and yelled, "Keep it up, Mr. Brown, I like that! You're gonna' go places someday!" I guess Mr. Shaffer, my arithmetic teacher, and my nameless (I hated his ass) music teacher couldn't see or hear what I was trying to do.

They wanted me to suck up to them like most of the other kids or they'd make fun of me as a "bad example" by threatening my classmates with "do as I say or you'll end up like that loser Larry Brown". I'd heard that crap all my life and in the end, it was dear Mr. Talbot, a black teacher who had to stay invisible most of the time to keep his job, who was the first to "see" my potential and to encourage me to continue to do something with it.

I also found refuge in the pages of *Reader's Digest*. I loved reading the "Quotable Quotes" and the short stories. My vocabulary expanded as I took the "Word Power" test. I didn't know it then, but in more ways than one, *Reader's Digest* would change my life and help me become a better songwriter when I needed the perfect word to finish a lyric. Uncle Joe's house also became a sanctuary for all us Brown kids.

He served the best lamb chops I ever ate and the only payment he required was my attendance at Temple, as the tenth man for the Minion, to say Kaddish, which are the prayers for the dead. In the Jewish faith, a minion requires ten men, thirteen years or older. I was honored and so happy to see how proud Uncle Joe was to have me with him at such special moments. Joseph London was my great uncle, my father's mother's brother, and the assistant postmaster of Newark. How we all loved him! The love Uncle Joe showed me turned out to be the second -time God reached out His Hand to save me. Though I did not know it, or realize it at the time, He had already given me the Grace of connecting with my Jewish family at Jamesburg, and again through my beloved uncle. May God rest his beautiful soul.

* * * *

Later, I took most of the life lessons I learned in elementary school and at the State Home for Boys to South Side High School. The first thing I figured out was that I didn't want to be there. What they learned about me was that I would only attend for two out of the eight weeks I was scheduled to be there. I was issued a trumpet in my music class and my assignment was to learn to play a musical scale. I wanted to play something else.

Mr. Landolphi, the principal, asked me why I had been absent for six of the eight weeks I was enrolled at the school. "What's the problem, Larry? You've been absent for over a month!" I told him the teachers were boring and the place smelled like spoiled milk. He erupted, "Don't come back here until you have a note from your father assuring me that you will do better". The school sent letter after letter to my house looking for me and although my father had the only key to the mailbox, I had a screwdriver. Another message The Weed missed.

My final day at South Side High, I came into class, put my foot on my chair, held the mute to the front of the horn, and doing my best Harry James impersonation, played the opening lines to "Tenderly". The class went wild! So, did the teacher. He ripped the horn out of my hands and sent me to the principal's office.

Chapter 4

A -WOP-BOP-A-LOO-BOP-A-WOP-BAM-BOOM!

The country's heady World War Two sense of accomplishment, joy, and freedom led us down a musical path no one saw coming or could stop. This new music with its blend of soul born out of Africa (brought over with the slaves, and first heard in the cotton fields of the deep South) was unshackling the traditional popular music when it was mixed with country music. Combining the two created a new, rebellious sound, born out of poverty, and uniquely American.

There wasn't a moment that music of one kind or another wasn't playing in the Brown madhouse. My early "music teachers", that is the big-name stars, were

Bing Crosby (1903-1977), Al Jolson (1886-1950), and Rosemary Clooney (1928-2002). It's important you know a little about who they are- "A friend nicknamed Harry Crosby *Bingo*, which was later changed to *Bing*, for his love of an illustrated parody newspaper called *The Bingville Bugle*."[9] "Al Jolson was born Asa Yoelson in Lithuania. He was known in the industry as *The World's Greatest Entertainer,* for well over 40 years."[10]

After his death, his influence continued unabated with such performers as Sammy Davis Jr., Elvis Presley, Mick Jagger, David Bowie, Jackie Wilson and Jerry Lee Lewis, who all mentioned him as an inspiration". "Rosemary Clooney was born on May 23, 1928, in Maysville, Kentucky. She sang and toured with a big band in the 1940s and eventually signed with *Columbia Records* as a solo artist. Her first No. 1 hit was "Come On-a My House" in 1951. In the 1950s, she starred in the movie *White Christmas* with Bing Crosby and had her own television show.[11]

---
9 Bing Crosby's Life and Career, PBS.org, http://www.pbs.org/wnet/americanmasters/episodes/bing-crosby/timeline-bing-crosbys-life-and-career/3501/
10 Al Jolson, IMBD Biography, http://www.imdb.com/name/nm0427231/
11 Rosemary Clooney Biography, (1928-2002), Bio, http://www.biography.com/people/rose-

Another "teacher" was my namesake, Russ Columbo (1908-1934), who met his end with a bullet to his head. Supposedly it was an accidental death, then again . . . His life is summed up this way, "Russ Columbo was born on January 14, 1908 in Camden, New Jersey, USA as Ruggiero Eugenio di Rodolfo Colombo . . . A major romantic idol in the early 1930s, was in the midst of a highly-publicized romance with Carole Lombard (which her studio was said to have strongly opposed) when he was killed in a bizarre shooting 'accident' at the age of 26".[12]

The circumstances of Russ Columbo's sudden death, if true, constitute one of the most freakish freak accidents ever brought to popular attention. Here is what one source says, "The story as it is most frequently given runs thus: Columbo was visiting the studio of a photographer friend when the friend, in lighting a cigarette, lit the match by striking it against the wooden stock of an antique French dueling pistol. The flame set off a long-forgotten charge in the gun, and a lead pistol ball

mary-clooney-9251425
12 Russ Columbo Biography, IMDB, http://www.imdb.com/name/nm0173375/bio

was fired".[13]

My favorite radio station, WNEW, featured the voice of America's number one DJ, Guillermo "William" B. Williams, (1923-1986), who was the first to refer to Frank Sinatra as the "Chairman of The Board". WNEW was still broadcasting the music I loved best. These were inspirations to me in the form of the music and lyrics of Cole Porter (1891-1964), Irving Berlin (1888-1988), Sammy Cahn (1913-1993), and Jimmy van Heusen (1913-1990), who wrote so many of Sinatra's classics. But, as much as I liked the new sounds, I hadn't completely converted to the new music taking the US by storm. William B's radio program, "The Make-Believe Ballroom" was still my reality.

In the early 50's, the constant beat of R&B music being broadcast 24/7 from WNJR was something you couldn't get anywhere else and Rock n' Roll was just around the corner. Little Richard (born Richard Penniman in 1932), Chuck Berry (1926-2017), Bo Diddley

---
13 IBID.

(born Elias Bates, 1928-2008) and the electrifying, Jackie Wilson (1934-1984), still send chills through me when I hear versions of "Higher and Higher". They were breaking the sound barrier and the explosions could be heard on the streets of the city.

The early radio station DJs were pioneers. They programmed their own music and played whatever turned them on. They were self-appointed guardians of the sound of their stations-completely devoted to the music and undying fans of the artists they helped promote to stardom. Their love and dedication for this new music led them to discover the magic 'B' side of the single 45 rpm records they were being asked (paid or bribed) to play. They were the piped pipers in tune with the new army of fans reshaping the tastes and fortunes and ultimate destiny of the record companies.

Alan Freed (1921-1965), the legendary radio DJ and now member of the Rock n' Roll Hall of Fame, who called himself *Moon-dog*, christened the new music "Rock n' Roll". Danny Stiles (1923-2011), a young, hip

Jewish DJ known as *The Catman* worked for WNJR, the R&B (rhythm and blues) radio station that broadcasted out of Union, New Jersey to the New York metropolitan area with Hal Jackson (1915-2012), his black alternate on the station.

They introduced R&B music to young black and white audiences hungry for something new in the early 1950s. I didn't know he was white until I met him several years later when I brought him my first single release, a rockabilly song that didn't fit his radio station format, but he played it anyway.

They introduced the world to such classic 'B' sides as "Rock Around the Clock" by Bill Haley and the Comets, "Tequila" by the Champs, "Be-Bop-a-Lula" by Gene Vincent, "I'm Sorry" by Brenda Lee, "Save the Last Dance For Me" by the Drifters, "Green Onions" by Booker T. and the MGS, "Unchained Melody" by The Righteous Brothers, "Ruby Tuesday" by the Rolling Stones, "Sunny" by Bobby Hebb (1938-2010), and "Love Me Do" by the Fab Four, and there were so many more.

We heard the new sounds blasting out of cars, like a '54 Hudson Hornet with the tops coming down faster than a prom girl's dress. We were young studs doing 'The Fish' with dreamy, sweet smelling teenage girls, who knew the reason we learned how to dance. We could move in tight and hold them around their waists, grinding to those beautiful, soulful songs "Earth Angel", "In the Still of The Night", and "My Prayer", by the incomparable 'Platters.

We felt something deep inside Pat Boone and Doris Day couldn't touch. We felt the beat, the words, so simple, and yet so powerful. Those gorgeous, amazingly catchy melodies sung by some of the greatest singers ever born; recording them in one take, no second chances, no punch ins, no computers, and no auto tune. In those days, what you got was what the singers actually recorded.

Today, what we hear on the radio is often the final retakes or computer enhanced re-recordings of the acts or musicians to correct pitch, performance, phrasings, and other problems. In the old days, none of that equipment existed, so the great recordings were great because of the amazing talent of the acts and musicians, not the equipment that can make them sound better.

Those agonizingly beautiful vocal performances were prying us loose from our shells and connecting us like nothing ever did. The connection is still with me and all of us who lived in those times, listening to those 'oldies but goodies' still rings true. Tight skirts and sweaters, and all that pink lipstick answered the question, "I wonder if she's into it?" She was. We could see right through them as they were shaking and shimmying to "Get A Job" by the Silhouettes.

Guys danced, we had to. It was ok to show off the steps you knew, it was 'cool, "Cool as a Moose!" We learned how to dance by watching the kids on American Bandstand. The 'regulars' whose names were as familiar to us as our best friends in school, Justine and Bob, Kenny and Arlene. Thanks for the free lessons!

It came as no surprise that DJs like *Murray The K* (Murray Kaufman 1922-1982) referred to himself as the fifth Beatle. These guys were possibly the most influential disc jockeys of all time. They were the first to introduce live shows integrating black, white, and Latino artists on the same stage, long before the start of the Civil Rights movement. I was fifteen years old when God, disguised as a twenty-year old kid from Tupelo, Mississippi, appeared on the *Tommy Dorsey TV Show*. "Dorsey (1905-1956) was a popular American trombonist who performed with brother Jimmy in the Dorsey Brothers Orchestra during the 1920s and '30s. He was bandleader of the Tommy Dorsey Orchestra in the 1930s and '40s."[14]

I was in Uncle Joe's house when I first saw the 'King'! The next day I bought a Silver Tone electric guitar at Sear's and in ten days taught myself how to play, "That's Alright Mama". I wanted to be Elvis! I grew

---

14 Tommy Dorsey Biography, Conductor, Trombone Player, Bio http://www.biography.com/people/tommy-dorsey-9277676,

sideburns, turned my collar up, walked, talked, and copied his every move. It seemed like everybody else was doing it, too. I bought all of his records and wore them out on my old Victrola record player singing and dancing along with him.

Music was "groovy" back then. It was the driving force in our lives. The pace and style of our conversation, the excitement created by every new song, the energy flowing out of our rock idols, was intoxicating, infectious, and affordable. All of that excitement from a 45 rpm (revolutions per- minute), single vinyl recording for less than a dollar! And it scared the crap out of our parents. Girls were staging 'make out' parties (disguised as dance parties) in the basements of their houses and they were growing increasingly more curious, more promiscuous.

Teenage pregnancies were on the rise as girls were being driven crazy wondering what was too little to give and what was too much. Moral codes and values established and presided over by the Church and solidified by the movies of the 40's and 50's were being subverted now by the exposure kids were getting to our most primitive and provocative instincts. Those new preachers of rock an' roll, these young heathens, were selling "SEX!"

Another bizarre screaming genius now moved us. He had every teenager changing gears. Elvis is forever the *"King of Rock n' Roll"*. But Little Richard, whose antics and deliberate, provocative use of lipstick and eye makeup applied to accentuate his expressions of wonder and delight (that made him look like he was plugged into a socket from outer space), with his screams of "Whoooo", shaking his head like he was possessed by the devil; he was the *"Queen" of Rock n' Roll*.

How could the lyrics of Little Richard's "A-WOP-BOP-A-LOO-BOP-A-WOP-BAM-BOOM!" compete with "Hey there, you on that high-flying cloud, though he won't throw a crumb to you, you think someday he'll come to you, better forget him, him with his nose in the air, he has you dancing on a string, break it and he won't care?"

A true minister (as he would later become) of this new religion, crying out, screaming out, coming out for his legion of devoted followers were young acts who would keep the faith; musicians who would copy his 'licks' and moves. We know some of those young acts today as The Beatles, The Rolling Stones, and so many other legendary artists of the 60's, 70's, 80's and beyond. Though I couldn't relate to Little Richard at first, in 1971 at a BMI Country Music Award Dinner in Nashville, I ran up to him, told him I loved him, and kissed his ring!

Chapter 5

My First "Hit"

If it weren't for music, I'd be dead or probably be selling hot dogs in the Witness Protection program with John Tully. Thank God, I've never had to put my hands into cold water. After my release from the State Home for Boys, my father would not allow me to hang out with any of the boys I had previously gotten into trouble with.

So, I formed a new friendship with two guys from the projects who were into music (as opposed to other people's property). We practiced up on the rooftops of the projects. Dick Lebo, a future Newark police officer, played drums on a cardboard box, Richard, "The Ox", Oxman on guitar, and me on my harmonica. Together, we wrote our first song "Spooky Rock". I was creating a new reality for myself and as long as I stayed inside my head, writing and creating, I somehow knew it would lead me to a better life.

We also liked to hang out at Syd's over on Chancellor Avenue, across the street from Weequahic High School. After reading this description, I bet you can see why we liked it- "In 1941, Syd Goldstein, whose family was in the dairy business in Bayonne, bought a small restaurant at 340 Chancellor Avenue between Summit Avenue and Hobson Street, near Weequahic High School . . . He renamed it "Syd's" and introduced a menu that featured hot dogs and hamburgers, but also included Rolled Beef, Ham, Cheese Sandwiches, Tuna and Egg Salad, and Potato and Kasha Knishes . . . Earlier in 1941, you could buy a hot dog at Syd's in two sizes: three cents or six cents".[15]

The luncheonette was honored by the *Newark Star Ledger* in 1956 as having "the best hot dog in New Jersey".[16] Syd's was a teenage hangout that looked like a movie set from films like *American Graffiti, Rebel Without a Cause,* and the popular TV show about life

---
15 Syd's Hot Dogs: History of a Weequahic Landmark by Nat Bodian, Old Newark Memories, http://www.oldnewark.com/memories/weequahic/bodiansyds.htm
16 IBID.

in the 1950s, *Happy Days*. It was 'THE' hangout. You ordered an MK (mustard and sauerkraut) or an MO (mustard only), Naked (just the dog), or SW (sweet works-mustard, sweet relish, and sauerkraut). My favorite was a HWK, hot works with 'kraut-hot relish and mustard. We had code before there was "LOL" and "OMG".

There was always a crowd of teenage girls wandering around flirting with sweaty boys who were coming off Untermann Field, a playground located across the street and adjacent to the high school. The jukebox never stopped. A nickel got you a spin of "At the Hop" by Danny and the Juniors. I can still hear those songs swirling around in my head. I remember watching Elvis 'look a-likes' hitting on the cutest blonde twirlers and cheerleaders from school. The way they looked at me, wearing my ripped jeans and a dirty T-shirt, I knew none of them wanted to be with me. If they were ever gonna' want me, I would have to be the voice they were moving to that was coming out of the jukebox.

School was out, now it was just me and 'The 'Ox'. We had become a duet. We wrote songs and performed them at The Asbury Park Convention Center. We called ourselves "The Duals" and one day we decided it was time for "The Duals" to get serious. "Wait Up Baby" was one of the first songs we ever recorded.

It led us on a trip to a bizarre episode with Bobby Robinson (1917-2011), the first redheaded black man either one of us had ever seen. We were young teenage Everly Brothers 'wannabes' soon to be rejected by just about every record company in Manhattan. I convinced Ox that we should head up to Harlem. I was determined to find the record company that I knew was headquartered there. We couldn't get arrested downtown, so one hot August night we took the infamous 'A Train' uptown to 125th Street.

We passed *Bobby's Record Shop*, a two by four little R&B record store with a giant speaker on the sidewalk, blaring out, what the preachers railed against as the devil's music! I remember thinking how odd it was to see white men 'prophets of doom' standing on milk crates, preaching the word of God to a predominantly black community as disinterested in them as we were.

It was the music coming out of the store that got our attention, but was this the record company headquarters? We checked the address, could it be? Carrying our guitars, Ox and I squeezed inside and asked the redhead, "Are you Mr. Robinson? Is this Fury Records?" He said, "Yeah, this is it". We told him who we were. He didn't seem to care much. But when we asked if we could play our song (sensing that we were determined to carry this out to its ultimate, albeit, questionable, conclusion), he smiled and said, "Go for it, boys".

We ripped into "Wait Up Baby". As he was watching us, studying us, I knew what he was thinking, "two crackers in my store in Harlem, they must be crazy". But damned if they ain't good!" We made an impression all right. I could see it by the look on his face. He cared now! He smiled again, a smile of appreciation for our music or maybe just for our sheer guts in coming to Harlem to audition for him. The guy who would give us our first deal had quite a story,

> Robinson during World War II was an Army Corporal stationed in Hawaii . . . .in charge of coordinating entertainment for soldiers awarding to be shipped off to battle in the Pacific by hiring big bands, singers and even a one-legged tap dancer. But Robinson made a killing on the side as a loan shark . . . saving over $8,000 in the interest he charged to servicemen . . . In 1946, he became the first colored man to open his own shop on 125th Street . . . In the 1950s, he became one of the first Harlem entrepreneurs to seize on the doo-wop street culture, forming Red Robin and Whirlin' Disc record labels. In the 1960s, he discovered Gladys Knight & The Pips and produced King Curtis on a new label Enjoy Records.[17]

He said that he loved our sound and that he owned the record company and was ready to sign us to a worldwide label deal, "Right Now!" "You serious? You mean it?" He reassured us. We were ecstatic. This was real confirmation. The head of a record company loved us! A chance at stardom! We couldn't hide our excitement. We were thrilled to death. We left Harlem that night thinking it was the most beautiful place on earth

---
17 Bobby Robinson (1017-2011); An Unreleased History, by Dan Charnas, http://www.dancharnas.com/2011/01/bobby-robinson-1918-2011-an-unreleased-history/

and the following week we went back to sign a record contract with his partner, 'Fats', the money man.

I remember the day I first met the 'fat man'. At the instruction of Robinson, we proceeded to a beautiful brownstone located two doors from Central Park. A lady let us in and told us to go downstairs to the basement. We saw a note on top of a stack of papers on the edge of the most elaborately decorated stone and brass bar we had ever seen. It read, "Sign all papers where indicated!" We did, we signed them all. Even where our names didn't appear.

A few minutes later a deep voice growled out, "Did you sign the papers?" I immediately climbed back up the stairs to find the voice that was coming from the bathroom. "Did you sign that contract, boy?" I peered in and there, standing naked, except for the white mound of shaving cream on his face, stood a giant black figure. Wide eyed, I answered, "Yes sir, we both signed it". He said, "Good, I'll be right down, wait for me there". Suddenly, everything I had been programmed to believe about blacks not knowing much just went out the window. Which is where Ox and I would have been thrown, if we hadn't put our 'John Hancock' (our signatures) on those papers.

"Wait Up Baby" sold two records. Maybe!

Chapter 6

The Weed

My father liked to make a bet or two and was always dressed to the nines. He smelled like a bottle of Old Spice and looked like a million bucks when he went out. He even changed his outfit several times a day. For a man who had a hard time paying the rent, he always managed to look like he owned the building. He had an eye for the ladies and they liked him too. With black, naturally curly hair (and except for a slightly larger than normal proboscis) I have to admit, he was a strikingly handsome man. It was only a matter of time before it would all come home to roost. Late one night someone knocked on our door. I answered it and a fierce looking Filipino, Dotty Tanela's husband, told me "Go, get your father!"

Dotty was a pretty young woman with whom the old man had been having one of his dalliances. They knew it . . . now, apparently . . . so, did her angry husband! I called out to The Weed that someone was here to see him and when he stepped in front of the door the Filipino coldcocked him. He came right back at the guy with a flurry of punches and they grappled with one another, tumbling down the concrete stairs-landing at the base of the door on the ground level.

They kept bashing the hell out of each other, and, as bad as he'd been to me, I had to stop it. I quickly found my mom's rolling pin, ran down the stairs but couldn't hit either, as they wouldn't stop moving. Finally, somebody heard the screams and yelled for help.

Rumbling down from the third floor came Mrs. Lewis. Madge Lewis was a towering Scotswoman, who was at least six feet tall and weighed well over two hundred pounds. She grabbed both of them by the backs of their shirts and separated them like little kids. She yelled at

Mr. Tanela to "get the hell out of there" and told my old man to "go back to his apartment".

Tanela got the hell out of there and my father, nose bleeding and lip bloodied, turned and thanked Mrs. Lewis. As you can see, there was never a dull moment in the housing projects and it was usually my old man who was right in the center of it.

Mr. Lewis, who was even bigger than his wife, was a giant of a Scotsman who worked at the A&P. He always seemed to be on the 'sauce' . . . the kind you don't spread over 'Haggies' or 'Stovies'. An uneducated man, with all the prejudice and intolerance that goes with it, he used to walk past our window muttering anti-Semitic slurs.

One day, my father, who happened to be good friends with a group of Italians and Jews, who were, let us just say, "connected", had a conversation about Mr. Lewis and his vile remarks. Abe used to play softball in Elizabeth with the hard guys from the projects; and, like Jake Mohawk from Hawthorne Avenue, they also took his "action" when he wanted to bet on the ponies or a fight.

He told one of the 'good fellas' about the problems he was having with Mr. Lewis. One night, about a half-dozen of the "connected characters" with The Weed following behind them, ran up the stairs to the third floor and banged on Mr. Lewis's door. When he opened it, they pulled him to the ground, shoved a pistol in his mouth, and in no uncertain terms told him, "If you ever so much as look at our friend Abe Brown again, it'll be the last time you see anybody. You got that?" Lewis was crying-begging, "I'm sorry. I'm sorry. I'll never do it again". They pulled the gun out of his mouth and left him there on his knees, shaking.

The Weed had a lot of faults but drinking wasn't one of them. He couldn't hold his liquor so he rarely touched the stuff. One night he was walking home and had to pass Jaymar's Tavern. A voice rang out from inside the bar, "Abe!" He peered inside and to his surprise, it was Mr. Lewis beckoning him to come in. It was time to make the peace.

My father accepted the offer of a drink, and another, and a few hours later a 'Giant', with a sack of The Weed slung over his shoulder, came walking home. They were finally singing the same tune. He deposited my father on the couch, gave him a kiss on the cheek and went up to his apartment. The old man just about made it to the bathroom where he lingered over the bowl for an hour. From that day on, they were the best of friends.

It's strange how once people come to know each other we often become friends. As an example, Mr. Lewis was home the day my sister, Annette, and Dinah Lewis, the Lewis's oldest daughter, were playing on a railing in the stairwell between the second and third floor. My sister had a penny in her mouth as she hung upside down on the railing and the penny got stuck in her windpipe. She was turning blue and about to choke to death when just by sheer coincidence Mr. Lewis stumbled into them. He picked up Annette, turned her upside down and slapped her on the back. The penny popped out! God Bless Mr. Lewis for making peace with my father; he saved my sister's life.

Soon after that incident, I learned that my father wanted to be a health inspector. Imagine that! I remember him threatening me if I didn't help him take the exam. I diligently drilled him on the questions. He was an educated man, although he must have been playing 'hooky' when they taught classes on "civility", "human decency", and "kindness". He passed the test with flying colors. He thanked me by forgetting to bat me around for a week or two. Things began to get better for us after my father became a Health Inspector for the City of Newark. I still have his badge tucked away in a drawer somewhere.

Chapter 7

A Leap of Faith

I was about to turn 16 and I needed a change. I was tired of getting beaten up by The Weed and put down by my teachers. There was a big world out there, full of mountains, deserts, rivers, another ocean, and I wanted to see all of it. So, with a nickel in my pocket and the clothes on my back, I walked across the park to Highway 29 (later renamed Route 22, the most dangerous highway in the Garden State), and started hitchhiking to California.

The police stopped me in Phillipsburg, New Jersey, and phoned my mother. I begged her not to make them bring me home. She told them to let me go! The next person to give me a ride told me he needed to stop to get some gas and a bite to eat. He asked me if I was hungry and I told him, "No." Then he asked me if I had any money and I told him, "No", again. He insisted I have something to eat and he would pay for it. We ate and he drove me up the highway and when he dropped me off, he insisted on giving me ten dollars.

By the time I got to the middle of Pennsylvania, I had eaten about six meals and had over a hundred bucks stashed in my shoes. I got picked up by another young man who asked me where I was going. "California", I responded. He asked me when was the last time I had eaten and I told him, "Yesterday".

He was on the way to the store to get some formula and medicine for his sick baby. He didn't have much to offer, but he insisted on buying me something to eat. "Take this", as he shoved his last couple of bucks into my hand. I was mortified, guilt ridden. I tried to refuse his charity, but he would have none of it. I put the money in my pocket and choked on my third breakfast of the morning. After he drove off, I walked down the highway feeling as guilty as I had ever felt in my life.

Outside of Pittsburgh I got a ride with two hysterical guys who drove me all the way to Salt Lake City. They had a pet hamster in a cage behind the back seat and it kept running on its little wheel all the way to Utah. I went south after that and caught a ride with a young, powerful looking man, who told me he was going as far as Phoenix. It was hot and getting late so I thought "what the hell". He bought a six-pack and drove into the middle of nowhere for at least fifty miles. I watched the sun slowly disappear over a distant mountain range, and started to notice that it was getting pitch black outside the trucks windows.

Suddenly, he pulled about two hundred yards off the highway and drove into the desert. I started to feel unnerved, uneasy, as I didn't think this was the local detour to Phoenix. He parked the truck, got out, and motioned to me to join him and have a beer. I told him I didn't drink. He smiled, "That's ok, kid, jump out, c'mere, I'll have one for you, too". I got out and watched him open a can of beer with one of those old-metal can openers that he tossed back onto the front seat. I glanced up at the blazing stars in the clear desert sky, as it was a glorious sight. I had never seen the sky look so beautiful.

My being lost in the moment became his chance to attack. He grabbed me from behind, put his arm around my neck, choking me, tighter, tighter. I could see a bright white light in my head getting brighter with every breath. There was no color left in my brain, his hold was too strong. I was rapidly losing oxygen. Just before I started to black out I realized this bastard was trying to kill me. I found the strength to lift the right heel of my cowboy boots and smash it into his genitals. He hollered in pain and fell backwards. I ran to the open door on the truck and grabbed the beer can opener he had left on the front seat. Clenching it in my right hand, I told him if he came towards me I was going to tear his eyes out.

He made an attempt to apologize. "I was just trying to test your reflexes, just kidding around". "Fuck you", I told him, "my father's a Marine and a Judo expert and he taught it to me, too. If you make another move you're gonna' get killed". Of course, that wasn't true, but it sounded good at the time.

I thought of stealing his truck and leaving him in the desert, but I had been there and done that and all that got me was years of cleaning urinals and toilets in the State Home for Boys at Jamesburg. Holding the can opener to his face, I jumped back in the front seat and ordered him to do the same. I told him "drive and don't look at me. "If you do, you mother fucker, I'm going to tear your eyes out!"

We rode until daybreak and when we reached what appeared to be downtown Phoenix, we stopped at an intersection. The town was deadly still. Before the light turned green, I jumped out and ran down the street. I hid under a car and didn't move for what seemed like an eternity, holding my breath, until I was sure he was gone. My body was shaking. I had just cheated death. Hitchhiking took on a new meaning. 'My next ride could be my last'. But with no other option at hand, I stuck out my thumb again.

I caught a ride to Los Angeles where my uncle Arthur, my mother's brother lived. He welcomed me into his home. He had always been there for me when he lived in Newark. I remember hiding at his house for three days, when I was younger. My father had chased me over the rooftops of the projects, after beating me again, and again, after I had told him to "go fuck himself".

Uncle Arthur finally brought me home and told my father if he ever hurt me again he would kill him. The old man never hit me again. My Uncle Arty, my Guardian Angel, what would I have done without him?

Ok, been there, done it. I felt the waters of the cold Pacific Ocean running through my toes as I walked the beach, ate an orange I picked from an orange tree, escaped certain death from a nut in the desert-that was enough. It was time to go home. But my curiosity got the best of me again. I wasn't completely satisfied. I'd read about discrimination problems in the South, and wanting to see what it was all about for myself, I took the southern route home.

It took me three days to get through Texas. I thought I was going to die in the heat waiting for a ride that never seemed to come. I watched truck after truck filled with migrant Mexican workers going out to the fields and coming back in, and still no ride.

A ride finally came and I was on my way to Louisiana. A few days later, I found myself walking into the small town of Eutaw, Alabama. A much nicer place today than when the KKK was around, as can be determined here,

> The town of Eutaw . . . was created on December 13, 1819 and was originally known as Mesopotamia. In 1838 . . . the city agreed to change its name to Eutaw to honor the Revolutionary War victory . . . In 1870, the town was the site of . . . the Eutaw Riot, in which a large group of disaffected black Republican voters were attacked by a party of white men belonging to the Ku Klux Klan.[18]

Standing in front of the gas station I saw a young black kid pumping gas. I approached him, but after fielding too many questions from me about the current racial conditions, he grew increasingly nervous and asked me to stop. He told me he couldn't talk to me anymore. "Why?" His answer rocked me to my knees. "Because

---
[18] Eutaw, Encyclopedia of Alabama, by Claire M. Wilson, Auburn University. http://www.encyclopediaofalabama.org/article/h-2501

we could both get killed, that's why". I could see the fear in his eyes. He was so young, so frightened and suddenly, so was I. I had heard that racially motivated killings were becoming more commonplace than ever in the South. I had read about Emmet Till, a young black man who had been murdered in 1955, for allegedly flirting with a white woman. Everyone seemed to be scared to death; this seemed to be no place for a white boy to be hanging around asking questions that were none of my business. But somehow, I felt that it was my business.

I finally made it home but started to think maybe The Weed wouldn't let me come back after my adventure. I was wrong. I was at Uncle Joe's house when he called and told me to come home. He treated me differently after the trip. I guess I had made my point. I could take care of myself, and who knows, he may have even missed me. Soon after my return, I was playing Scrabble with a few of my friends when somebody began pounding on the door. They told me my mom and father were having a horrible fight. I ran to our apartment. My mom had an iron in her hand and The Weed had a bottle in his.

They were cursing at one another with my sisters and brothers shaking and crying on the sofa. Horrified, I grabbed the iron from my mother's hand and the bottle from his. I told them "Shut the fuck up" and to go into separate rooms. "If I hear another word from either one of you, you're going to be sorry!" I meant it and they knew it. One thing was certain, The Weed knew not to mess with me anymore. I was sixteen, bigger than him, and maybe tougher too. I'd had enough of the anger. Enough of the insanity that terrified my defenseless sisters and brothers. It had to end now and I wouldn't stand for it anymore. And the Weed knew it.

Chapter 8

Attention!

Each time I tried enlisting in the army they wouldn't take me. I told the truth about my problems and my stay at the State Home for Boys where I learned how to clean urinals and toilets. I was denied entrance. So, the next time I tried to enroll, I lied. I contracted a severe case of memory loss and was soon accepted into the United States Army. I took the oath and was told to come back in two days to ship out.

The ride to Ft. Dix, New Jersey, took about an hour and a half. Along with a group of other recruits, I was given boots, fatigues, and inoculated against diseases I didn't know existed. Then, I was issued orders for basic training at Ft. Hood, Texas. We were driven by bus to the Newark Airport where we had a four-hour wait before our plane took off. If there is one lesson you'll learn in the service it's how to hurry up and wait. The Sergeant put me in charge. Why, I don't know. I guess he wanted someone familiar with the Newark area to babysit the others. He left us waiting for the plane. My house was close to the airport, so I called The Weed who came and we had something to eat.

When I got back, one of the new recruits asked me why I had not taken them for some food. I told him it was a family affair, which of course, pissed him off. He tried to retaliate when we arrived at the barracks at Ft. Hood. We were assigned to the same platoon. Our bunks were right beside one another. I made my bed, and began to sit down on the trunk, which contained our clothing and weapons.

This creep, who was much bigger than me, reached down and grabbed me by the lapels of my shirt and squeezed my neck. He ordered me to make his bed. We had been issued digging tools that came encased in heavy brown cloth. Mine were lying right on top of my trunk. I grabbed one by the handle and whacked him as hard as I could on the side of his face. As he smashed into the floor, I jumped on top of him and began to beat his brains in.

We were interrupted by Sergeant Solario (another S. O. B., whose name I'll never forget), "What the hell are you doing to this guy?" I told him, "Look sergeant, this guy is twice my size and he tried to beat me up". He said, "Brown, you look like a troublemaker to me and I'm going to ride your ass until you wish you weren't born!" And he did, non-stop for eight weeks.

One day, after a twenty-mile forced march, in what felt like 100-degree heat, (with full field pack and gear that weighed over twenty-five pounds), Sergeant Solario, who was standing in the shade, yelled. "Brown, get down and give me forty squat jumps". Holding my rifle above my head, I began jumping up and down-sweating bullets that I wanted to unload on that bastard. I got to the count of thirty and collapsed. A couple of other soldiers picked me up and carried me to my bunk.

Being the only "Yankee" in the platoon was a pain in the butt. Day after day for weeks on end the other guys rode my ass. I felt like an outcast. One night I went to the enlisted men's club and drank about a half dozen 3.2 beers. I was getting pumped up listening to the jukebox playing, "Sea Cruise", by Frankie Ford. I staggered back into the barracks stinkin' drunk and in a rage.

I climbed the stairs to the second floor and grabbed the first guy in the first bunk and punched him, screaming, "I'm ready to fight every one of you fuckers right now!" Before I knew it, several of them tackled me and hauled me to my bunk. They held my hands down and one of them put his fist to my face and said, "Brown, are you ready to go to sleep, or are you ready to go to sleep?" I nodded, and they let me go. I had earned the respect of the men in my unit.

Six weeks into basic training, one Sunday afternoon, I wandered into the enlisted men's club and heard a bunch of guys playing guitars and drums. I asked if I could sit in and play a little. They were playing rockabilly music. It was 1958 and Elvis was the rage. It felt so strange to know that he had been there. The "King!" Just like me! His signature was everywhere. He had walked the corridors, slept in a bed just like mine, peed in the same urinal, and maybe sang himself to sleep just like me. He had been through basic training in Ft. Hood, Texas. I had just missed him!

One of those good old' boys playing guitar looked at me and said with a deep southern drawl filled with sarcasm, "You play 'guitar', Brown?" I said, "Yeah, a little". He handed it to me and I started to play. I had been studying Elvis's records and I could finger pick like Elvis's guitar player, Scotty Moore. I could also do a mean imitation of Chuck Berry, with my hands running up and down the frets like greased lightning. I played and sang, "Roll Over Beethoven".

I went from worst to first with those guys. They looked at me in amazement and said, "Damn Brown, we never knew you could play like that!" I was one with them now and the last two weeks of my basic training were the best of the eight. I made more friends than I could shake a stick at and when basic training was over, we all left with handshakes and hugs!

My next assignment was to report to Ft. Gordon, Georgia. After a week of leave, which I spent back home in Jersey, I boarded the train at Penn Station in Newark. I took a seat next to another soldier in uniform. He was a young black man and we instantly hit it off. We stopped in Felice, a small town in the Carolinas, and we looked for a place to grab a bite. We sat down at the counter in a small shop in the train station.

A woman behind the counter looked at us and pointed to a sign that read, 'Coloreds' and told him he had to go around back to get his food. I protested, saying, "He's a soldier, look at his uniform". She shook her head and said, "Coloreds 'round back'." I got up and told him, "Let's get out of here". We walked a few blocks to a country store and bought bologna sandwiches and sodas and we ate them under a tree. I never marched in protests, never belonged to any organizations, but I could never accept any kind of discrimination.

Upon completing my course at Fort Gordon in Morse Code and typing, I attended graduation ceremonies. To add to the absurdity of the situation, they give me, a former Jamesburg alumni, a cosmic clearance with access to top-secret codes. Go figure! In case you aren't familiar with Morse code, here is a short description,

> The Morse code was difficult for most people to pass because the speeded-up tones flashed over the loudspeaker in the examination room sounded completely different, then the slow-pause tones Boy Scout toy oscillators made. "Kiddie" Morse code was taught in dots and dashes. Army Morse code was taught in dits and dahs. For example, in the Boy Scouts "SOS" sounded like "dot-dot-dot, dash-dash-dash, dot-dot-dot." In the Army, SOS sounded like, "dididit-dahdahdah-dididit".[19]

We were seated in alphabetical order. I found myself sitting next to my future writing and singing partner, Raymond Bloodworth. Before the ceremonies started they were playing rock n' roll music on the loudspeakers and I remember the song "I'm Gonna Get Married", by the great Lloyd Price. Raymond sang the first couple of lines and he sounded like Roy Orbison (1936-1988).

---
19 Cannon Fodder by Phillip Coleman, Chapter Four, Preparation, The Vietnam War Library, http://www.americanwarlibrary.com/a44/cf4.htm

I sang the next lines and, like in a Hollywood movie, we sang the last lines together.

At the conclusion of the graduation ceremony, we were given our orders to report to Ft. Dix. Bloodworth and I took the same plane to New Jersey and reported to camp. We were called by names in alphabetical order to receive our next assignments. Bloodworth received his orders, sat back down next to me and with his rich, Georgia drawl said, "Larry, you ain't gonna believe this one. I'm goin' ta' Paris, France". They called my name. I walked up to the soldier in charge, who looked at me, shook his head, and said, "You, lucky bastard. Here!" He shoved the papers at me and I saw the reason for his sarcasm. They read Shape Headquarters, Paris.

Chapter 9

Pigalle

It was 1958 and the cold war between the Soviet Union and the West was at its height. Camp Des Loges was a stonesthrow from Paris. SHAPE was close by-

> *Supreme Headquarters Allied Powers Europe (SHAPE) was established on 2 April 1951 in Rocquencourt, France, as part of an effort to establish an integrated and effective NATO military force . . . Fourteen months after the allies signed the North Atlantic Treaty the Korean war erupted in June 1950, increasing fears of a Soviet attack on Western Europe . . . Several countries were considered for the site of SHAPE's permanent HQ. However, countries in northern and southern Europe were considered too isolated from the rest of the command, Britain was not part of continental Europe and West Germany was not a NATO member and considered too close to Soviet-controlled territory . . . Therefore, General Eisenhower's staff recommended locating SHAPE in France because it was more central than other contenders. A site at Rocquencourt in the Versailles suburb of Paris was selected primarily because of the excellent communications it offered.*[20]

---

20 SHAPE in France, NATO/OTAN Allied Command Operations Supreme Headquarters Allied Powers of Europe, http://www.shape.nato.int/page134353332.aspx

Looking at our barracks it was hard to believe the conflict between the United States and the Soviet Union was heating up. The bunks were unmade, the place was a mess. As I started to I unload my things into my locker one of the guys said, "Don't do that. Nobody does nothing here. We've got it made. This place is like a country club. Relax, enjoy yourself and get ready for the time of your life".

Paris was only a thirty-minute bus ride. Some of the guys taught me how to drink and hold my liquor . . . European style. Most of us drank vodka as it's hard to smell on our breath and we didn't want the MPs (Military Police) to catch us tilted. I thought I knew a lot about women and something about life. But what I discovered in Paris earned me a doctorate in both subjects.

As a kid, I remember the first time I saw a naked woman was on the marquee of the Little Theatre, at the northern end of Broad (no pun intended), Street in downtown, Newark. I was 'south' of twelve years old and although I was too young to go inside, I could see by the leering looks on the faces of the derelicts and drunks who were constantly going into and out of the dive, I was missing out on something.

I asked the older woman (ticket taker) at the window "what was going on in there?" The lady at the window, looking sternly at me at first to be sure I was for real, told me with a wink to "Come back when you grow up, sonny. It's none of your business what's going on in there". I guess we both knew "what was going on in there!"

"Pigalle" was the local name for the red-light district that was 'open for all business'-legal prostitution post-World War Two in Paris, France. It had a reputation as follows,

> Soldiers during World War II nicknamed Pigalle, "pig alley" because of its seedy reputation, but it was actually named after the French sculptor Jean-Baptiste Pigalle (1714-1785), . . . Pigalle made his reputation with his acclaimed marble sculpture of Mercury (1741-2, Louvre; the terracotta model is in the Metropolitan Museum of Art, NY), which was shown at the French Academy of Fine Arts in 1744.[21]

---
21 "French Academy of Fine Arts Academie Royale de Peinture et de Sculpture." French Academy of Fine Arts: History, Salon Controversy. Accessed June 12, 2017. http://www.visu-

We got off the Metro at the Pigalle stop, climbed the grimy stairs only to find ourselves at the entrance to the world famous, Follies Bergere. The neon lights were blinding and the streets reeked with an odd combination of hot sausages and cheap perfume. I was hungry. But what should I have first? My priorities soon fell into line, which just happened to be a long line leading down the alleyways off of The Place, Pigalle. Each alley was lined by prostitutes saying, "Hey baby, baby, I can show you a good time". We all went up and down the lines trying to decide which menu item looked the best, and just like all the other guys I stopped as soon as I found what I was looking for.

* * * *

"Drop your pants, Brown, and lean against the wall. This is gonna' hurt!" It was the voice of Captain Hunt-the post doctor-as I remember it now-sounding a lot like Morgan Freemen in the movie, *The Shawshank Redemption*. Chuckling, he plunged the big needle carrying the penicillin into my quivering buttocks. Thirty

al-arts-cork.com/history-of-art/french-academy.htm.

minutes later, I could finally pee again! When I walked into the mess hall that night I heard one loud, 'Clap!'

My first three years in Paris were getting to me and I was scheduled to return home in about nine months when those damn Russians erected the Berlin Wall. Even the description of it now seems as complicated as it was in the moment-

> *West Berlin was a geographical loophole through which thousands of East Germans fled to the democratic West. In response, the Communist East German authorities built a wall that totally encircled West Berlin. It was thrown up overnight, on 13 August 1961 . . . The Berlin Wall (German: Berliner Mauer) was a barrier that divided Berlin from 1961 to 1989, constructed by the German Democratic Republic (GDR, East Germany) starting on 13 August 1961, that completely cut off (by land) West Berlin from surrounding East Germany and from East Berlin until it was opened in November 1989. Its demolition officially began on 13 June 1990 and was completed in 1992. The barrier included guard towers placed along large concrete walls, which circumscribed a wide area (later known as the "death strip") that contained anti-vehicle trenches, "fakir beds" and other defenses. The Eastern Bloc claimed that the wall was erected to protect its population from fascist elements conspiring to prevent the "will of the people" in building a socialist state in East Germany.*[22]

[22] The Berlin Crisis and the construction of the Berlin Wall, BBC History, http://www.bbc.

My Sergeant called me in and asked, "Specialist Brown, when are you scheduled to be discharged?" "In about nine months", I told him. He laughed, "I doubt that, trooper, you've been extended, indefinitely!" I was crushed. After three years of military duty in France, even with Paris so close by, I wanted to go home.

Bloodworth and I decided to put together a singing and dancing act called, "The Bug Outs". In a couple of months, we were charging over two hundred dollars a night, entertaining the brass in downtown Paris. I even remember a show we did for a couple of Generals. One night, we were booked to do our song and dance routine for General Louis Norstad and General 'True Blue' Walker, two of the highest-ranking officers in France. We were held up in heavy traffic and arrived more than an hour late. The generals were livid and told us they were only going to pay us half of our usual $200.00 a night fee. I told them, "$200 is our price". They glared at us, "You boys better be damned good". Bloodworth and I played, danced our asses off, and sang our hearts out and guess what, they paid us $200.00.

We later won a talent contest and the prize was a tour throughout Europe with the USO, one of the best ways we still support our troops -

> *The USO is a nonprofit, congressionally chartered, private organization, that relies on the generosity of individuals, organizations and corporations to support its activities. The USO is not part of the U.S. government, but is recognized by the Department of Defense, Congress and President of the United States, who serves as Honorary Chairman ... In 1941, as it became clear that the nation was heading into World War II, several organizations mobilized to support the growing U.S. military: The Salvation Army, Young Men's Christian Association, Young Women's Christian Association, National Catholic Community Services, National Travelers Aid Association and the National Jewish Welfare Board.[23]*

We entertained troops from Berlin to Verona. Gary Collins (1938-2012), who went on to become a famous television talk show host, was our master of ceremonies. It was a lot of fun playing so many different Army and Air Force bases in Europe. One day, during the

---
23 The USO, The Organization & History, http://www.uso.org/the-organization.aspx

tour, I disguised myself as a typical Berliner, brown pants, black tee shirt, black socks, and black shoes, and convinced another daring young soldier (who was on tour with us), to take the U-Bahn, the underground subway running from West to East Berlin. We got off the train at Alexanderplatz in the center of East Berlin and visited the shops and museums. This was a place rich in history:

> *Alexanderplatz or 'Alex' to Berliners, a cattle market in the Middle Ages, a military parade square and an exercise ground for nearby barracks until the mid 19th century - Alexanderplatz is the square named to honor Alexander I, Tsar of Russia, on his visit to Berlin in 1805. It was here that Alfred Döblin took the pulse of the cosmopolitan metropolis portrayed in his 1929 novel 'Berlin Alexanderplatz' filmed by Fassbinder for a TV series as a portrait of the bustling city in the 1920s before the imminent Nazi takeover. Fast forward to more recent times, one million people congregated here, on 4 November 1989 to demonstrate against the GDR regime shortly before the fall of the Berlin Wall. This was the largest anti-government demonstration in its history.[24]*

The church in the middle of the square was still in ruins and there were Russian soldiers in military vehicles ev-

---

24 Alexanderplatz berlin.de (English Version),https://www.berlin.de/orte/sehenswuerdigkeiten/alexanderplatz/index.en.php

erywhere. After about three hours of walking around, I began to get the creeps, realizing that if the Reds ever caught us with our dog tags on, we may spend the rest of our lives in the Gulag-the Soviet, forced labor camp system.

We boarded the U-Bahn and prayed that we would make it under the Brandenburg Gate, separating East and West Berlin. As we traveled on the subway, a Russian soldier was checking IDs. We just sat there, holding our breath; he never gave us a second look. When we got off the train in West Berlin, we both let out a huge sigh of relief. We had just dodged a very big bullet.

I was really growing tired of Europe, touring, and, I know it will sound odd, of Paris. I was sick of the nightlife, the hookers, the sleazy bars, the Smirnoff that I sipped on, falling all over myself, as I deposited the Russian liquid death on Pigalle's cobblestones. I craved something new and I found it at a small service club on the *Champs Elysees*, downtown Paris. That is where I rediscovered the reason why Paris inspires such great art and passion.

Chapter 10

The Juke Box

She was the daughter of the chauffeur of Spain's ambassador to France. With long, flowing black hair, tied back in a braid that ran down her milky white skin and eyes as black as coal, she pointed me in the direction that she wanted me to look. And she was just seventeen and you know what I mean. She was the hottest thing I had ever seen. We were at an Enlisted Men's Club, off the *Champs-Élysées*.

The *Champs-Élysées* sits in the northwest of Paris, France's capital, stretching from the Place de la Concorde down to the Place Charles de Gaulle where the *Arc de Triomphe* is-

> The *Champs-Élysées* were fields to begin with, filled with the gardens of merchants who sold their goods in Paris' local markets. In 1616, King Henry IV's wife Marie de Medici decided to clear the way for a tree-lined avenue in these fields that would extend from the Palais des Tuileries... By the later years of the 18th century,

> *the Champs-Élysées had gained a reputation for being a fashionable Parisian spot, as large houses and buildings erected along the avenue gave rise to impressive gardens and landscaping . . . By the 20th century, the Champs-Élysées had become a well-established Parisian center of commerce and culture as well as a source of national pride.*[25]

I spotted her talking to a local French girl. I introduced myself and after a few minutes of small talk, I asked her if she'd like to leave with me. Why wouldn't she? I was wearing my signature black leather jacket with the collar turned up and my hair slicked back, Elvis! It was an image that was foolproof. But somehow, this was different. She was different. She was so very young.

The women of Pigalle had nicknamed me, "Teddy Boy". In England, every kid (at that time) seemed to be an Elvis 'wannabe' and the girls called them *Teddy Boys*. I had entertained the hookers, night after night, singing and dancing on the tables in the local bistros.

But this was different. They had taught me well and I was going to teach her now. I led her to my favorite

---

[25] The History of Champs-Élysées by Laura Dixon, Demand Media, USA Today, Travel Tips, http://traveltips.usatoday.com/history-champs-elysee-14444.html

haunt and we ended up downstairs in an empty room beneath the bar. She said it felt hot down there and took off her sweater. Exposing my thoughts, I dropped all my francs into the jukebox and played "Twist and Shout", by the Isley Brothers "shake it up baby, twist and shout". She was moving now. I couldn't take my eyes off of her.

We danced in sync as if we had done it all our lives . . . wildly, for over an hour. "Come on come on, come on, baby, come on and work it on out". She loved to dance. I was nuts about her! She was a kid in one breath and a woman in the next. We danced, moving closer and closer.

There was no space between us now and we embraced. She wanted me. She started undressing-her body was incredible. I ripped my clothes off and she leaped into my arms and wrapped her legs around my waist, as I held her up against the jukebox, playing "shake it up baby". She rocked my world! What I was feeling then reminds me of a song I wrote later, called "Sock it To

Me, Baby!" recorded by *Mitch Rider and the Detroit Wheels*.[26] "Sock it to me", also became a featured bit with actress Goldie Hawn on the TV show *Laugh In*.

Sock
Oh, I'm so ready
Sock
Come on now, baby
Sock it
Honey in the beehive
Honeybunch, ha
Every time you kiss me
Hits me like a punch
Ready ready, ready, ready, ready
Ready or not
I want, yes I do, what you got
Sock it to me baby, baby
Sock it to me baby, baby
(Gotta) Sock it to me baby
Sock it to me, baby
Sock it to me, baby
Sock it
Boogaloo, my baby
Across the floor
Every time you shake it girl
I like it more
Gimme, gimme, gimme gimme gimme
Something sweet

Knock me
Ooh, off my feet
Sock it to me baby, baby
Sock it to me baby, baby
Sock it to me, baby
Sock it to me, baby
Sock it to me, baby
Sock it
Sock, baby
Sock it
Honey in the beehive
Honeybunch
Every time you kiss me
Hits me like a punch
Ready ready, ready, ready, ready
Ready or not
I want, yes I do, what you got
Sock it to me baby, my baby
Sock it to me baby, my baby
You've gotta sock it to me, baby
Sock sock it to me, baby
Sock it to me, baby
Sock it

Every night I was free I went downtown to be with her.

---
26 Mitch Rider and the Detroit Wheels musical recordings, "Sock it to Me Baby", by Bob Crewe and L Russell Brown, recorded (1967), New Voice Records

I was obsessed with her. We danced that dance night after night and it only got better. Thinking back to when I first arrived in Paris, I hated everything about the place. It was old and dirty. The people were distant and crass. The buildings were decaying and the language was impossible to understand. That all changed after Carmen. I fell in love with Paris, as I fell in love with her.

Not long after I had met Carmen there was an investigation of the officers that were running our unit. Most of them were court martialed and the ones who weren't were reassigned. Either way, I never saw any of them again. An entirely new group of 'gung-ho' NCOs (non-commissioned officers) had arrived at our unit and called us to roll call. Sergeant Ryder, with 'salad dressing' dripping down his chest, stood up on a milk crate and began to rip into us. It was a scene right out of a 'B' war movie.

He called us pieces of "worthless scum", and described the entire place as a garbage pit. He was going to make us into real soldiers again. We were going to work from dusk till dawn cleaning up the place. We'd be lucky if any of us ever saw Paris again! After his violent tirade, he paused, looked us over, and asked, "If there's anybody here that doesn't like me, or what I've said, raise their hand". One hand went up . . . mine.

I'd seen his type before, too much like my father, and I wasn't going to be pushed around by another sicko. He pranced over to me and with his nose right up against mine, screamed, "So you don't like me, soldier?" "No", I said. He yelled, "NO Sergeant!" I yelled back, "NO SERGEANT!" "That's better" was his response. Than he looked down at my khaki shirt, which bore my last name and said, "Brown, I'm gonna' ride you like a mule". "There won't be a day you don't wish I was dead". "You got that soldier?" I responded with a smirkie "Yes Sergeant". He screamed, "Get that shit eatin' grin off your face, and remember this wise ass, you'll never leave this post again while I'm in charge here".

It was torture being away from Carmen. But none of

us had any choice but to fall in line and do the work. We started in the Communications building filled with dangerous electronic wiring and metal slabs by covering all the wires with thick gray paint. But he wouldn't give up trying to make an example of me in front of the other men.

I was walking past the sergeant one day and he barked, "Get out of the fucking way, asshole". I yelled, "I don't have to take that shit from you", to which he roared back "I'm gonna' kill you!" I yelled out to the other soldiers nearby, "Sergeant Ryder said he's going to kill me". "You all heard it!" Ryder screamed, "Shut Up!" But I kept on yelling "this man just threatened to kill me". "You all heard him".

At that, the sergeant went into the captain's office just down the hall and both of them came out together. The captain and the sergeant were both "lifers" and they had another thing in common; they were both southerners, still fighting that uncivil war. The captain asked me what had happened. I told him I wanted to speak with Major Rink. I told him that the sergeant had just threatened to kill me.

The captain brought me into his office and tried to calm me down. After about ten minutes, he said, "Brown, everything's going to be ok now and you can forget about talking to the Major Rink, right?" My childhood anger from growing up in the Seth Boyden projects was building up in me. I replied, "I still want to speak with the Major". He exploded and told me that I was going to be court martialed for insubordination and lying about a recent 'bed count'. He said that one of the other soldiers who was not in his bunk one night was going to swear I had lied to cover for him. I said it was not true, but he proceeded to tell me, "We'll see about that, Brown" and he dismissed me.

A few days later, after the captain put in a request for a hearing with Major Rink, I was called into the Major's office. The Captain and Sergeant Ryder were already seated. The Captain ordered Sergeant Ryder to explain the charges against me. Major Rink then asked me to tell my side of the story. While I was answering the major's question, the captain wanted me to repeat something and I responded, "Let me reiterate".

He laughed and mockingly said, "Well, now, Specialist Brown is going to 'reiterate' for us". "Yes-I'm going to say it again for you, sir" and I repeated my statement. The Major then informed the Captain and Sergeant Ryder that he would take care of this himself. He dismissed them and after they left the room, he looked me in the eye and said, "Brown, you have less than six months to go in the army. Those two bastards have it in for you, so just mind your P's and Q's when you're around them. If they give you another problem, come and tell me about it. I'll straighten things out with them".

I thanked him and we ended up talking about Newark and the Bronx, where he was from. We discovered we had a lot in common. I felt relieved. Somehow there had always been someone looking out for me, Uncle Joe, Uncle Arthur, Mr. Rowe, and now, Major Rink.

A few days later, I was in the Communications building working and I got a sharp sliver of old dried up gray paint imbedded under my fingernail. I was in agony, trying to figure out how a piece of old paint could cause so much pain when Sergeant Ryder happened to walk by. He grabbed my hand and pulled the piece of hardened paint out from beneath my fingernail. Then, just as in Greek mythology's "Androcles and the Lion", without a word, he turned and walked away. I looked at my finger, and the pain was gone and so was my hatred for Sergeant Ryder.

One night, a couple of months before I shipped out of France, things further loosened up between the Sarge and me. I walked into the Communication's building to tell him that his car had been bashed in. He was the OOD (Officer of The Day), and looked a little tipsy. I asked, "Is everything all right, Sarge?" Holding his face in his hands he mumbled back, "My wife and I had a fight". I asked him what had happened to his car and he told me that he backed it into a cement block and then floored it into another one in front of him. I sat across from him, we had a long heart to heart, about - 'women!'

As we ended our "tete-a-tete" he said to me, "You know something Brown? Of all the men in this unit, if I were ever in a firefight again and I needed somebody to cover my ass, out of all the assholes in this unit, it would be you. You know why, 'cause I think you're crazy enough to shoot somebody".

I thanked him for the backhanded compliment, shook his hand, and thanked him for pulling that piece of paint out of my finger. He just smiled and I knew by the time our conversation was over, Sergeant Ryder and I were friends. No one except Raymond Bloodworth knew that Ryder and I had become friends until that fateful day at the bus stop. It was my last day at Camp Des Loges and Bloodworth and I were waiting with a few of our buddies at the bus stop saying our good-byes. Sergeant Ryder drove up in his car. He pulled over, jumped out, opened the back door, grabbed my duffel bag and threw it in the back seat. I jumped in front next to him and we sped off towards the train station in Paris. The guys' jaws dropping, they must have thought I was a double agent!

Carmen and I had already said our tearful good-byes and I promised I was coming back to marry her. She said, "I'll wait for you-come back to me, Brownie". The feelings of longing for Carmen reminds me of the song "Paradise" that I later wrote for Phoebe Cates which was used in the movie by the same name.[27]

In 1982, Joel Diamond, a successful record producer, called me to ask if I would come to his penthouse apartment on Central Park South to meet Phoebe Cates. She was a gorgeous, sensual teenager who had just finished filming the movie, *Paradise*. Joel wanted me to try and write the title song that hopefully, she would perform. She sang for me and, although it didn't hurt that she was 'drop dead' gorgeous, I loved the sound of her voice.

---

27 Phoebe Cates musical recording "Paradise" by Joel Diamond, and L. Russell Brown, (1992), Columbia Records, CBS/Sony

Could it be the little things you do to me
Like waking up beside you it's so new to me
Life can be so full of danger
In the dark there lurks a stranger
I just can't imagine what he wants of me
When I'm with you it's paradise
No place on earth could be so nice
Through the crystal waterfall
I hear you call
Just take my hand it's paradise
You kiss me once
I'll kiss you twice
As I gaze into your eyes
I realize it's paradise
It's right out of something from a fairy tale
A terribly exciting and a scary tale

It's nothing I could ever make up
Am I dreaming, will I wake up
Just to find out this is true reality
When I'm with you it's paradise
No place on earth could be so nice
Through the crystal waterfall
I hear you call
Just take my hand it's paradise
You kiss me once
I'll kiss you twice
As I gaze into your eyes
I realize it's paradise
Just take my hand it's paradise
You kiss me once I'll kiss you twice
As I gaze into your eyes
I realize it's paradise
As I gaze into your eyes
I realize it's paradise

Joel confided in me that this was a roll of the dice. He had no commitments from anyone to do a project. But he felt that we could get it "placed" if we could cut a great title song and maybe the score. I concocted a scheme. We made a demo of the "Paradise Theme" and to get approval from the movie producers to use the song in the movie, we went to Al Teller (the president of Epic Records). We told him we had a deal with the movie producers to use our song. Al looked at Phoebe's photo, he was drooling as he uttered, "You got an album deal!" We then returned to the movie producers and told them we had a record deal. They said, "Go for it!" Bingo!

Paradise was a hit movie abroad and our title song, "Paradise", became a huge hit. It was number 1 on the pop charts in Italy for several months. The melody is as familiar in Russia and other European Countries as "Yellow Ribbon" is in the United States. In 2003, another teenager, Kaci, had a two million selling dance version of "Paradise".

Back to 1962, I rode the train to Bremerhaven, Germany, where, along with hundreds of other soldiers, I boarded a troop ship bound for the good ole' U.S. of A. The harsh waves of the English Channel took their toll on most of the returning GI's. I didn't mind the rolling. It felt good to be going home-until I got sick from the smell of the upchuck from the guys who couldn't handle the rocking.

Chapter 11

Stupido

We dropped anchor less than a week later, in the shadow of the Statue of Liberty. I waited until the next morning to get off the ship and to receive my "honorable" discharge papers. My dear Aunt Virginia was waiting to drive me home from Brooklyn to Newark. I adored her. She was my mom's kid sister, and my first baby sitter.

I needed money and needed it fast as all I wanted to do was get back to Carmen. I found a job in an acid factory in the Ironbound section of Newark. It was a dangerous job, but I didn't care if it paid me well enough to get me back to my love in France. After about four months of exposure to the toxic chemicals, my ankles began to turn blue and I had to quit.

I wrote letter after letter to Carmen, but with no reply. I told myself "her family had probably gotten them and thrown them away". Of course, it was just the wishful, delusional thinking of a lovesick fool . . . me. I continued to scrimp and save enough money for a one-way ticket to Paris, and when I got it, I was on my way.

There was no stopping me now. In my letters to Carmen I had promised I would be at the *Arc de Triomphe* at a precise time. l was planning a romantic rendezvous, like the one I had seen in one of my favorite movies, *An Affair to Remember*. I was Cary Grant and Carmen, just as beautiful to me as Deborah Kerr, and we were about to replay this scene, or so I thought-

> *When the ship arrives in NYC, the lovers (Cary Grant and Deborah Kerr) are both engaged to others). They decide to make arrangements to meet at the top of the Empire State Building in 6 months if they both feel the same way about each other, and if Nickie (Cary Grant) can find a way to support the two of them in the manner they've become accustomed . . . But Terry (Deborah Kerr) never shows up (as) she is hit a taxicab (off screen) on the way to the meeting and is paralyzed. (Grant) tracks her down, as he's bitter and angry that she never showed up, but he wants to give her the shawl his grandmother left for her. Nickie (Grant) had sold one painting (to a woman in a wheelchair), makes the connection, finds the painting in Terry's (Kerr) bedroom and*

realized that she couldn't show up because of the accident.[28]

I arrived in Paris and waited at the *Arc de Triomphe* for what seemed like an eternity. Where was she? Had she forgotten . . . everything? Fear began to set in. I was frantic. I began searching the bars and service clubs. Playing a nagging, frightening hunch, I wandered into an officer's club on the *Champs 'Elysees*.

There she was, talking to a young Lieutenant. I walked towards her, and when she saw me, I could tell by the look on her face that I was right. She had never gotten my letters. She had given up hope that I would return, or that I would keep my promise. She threw her arms around me, gave me a hug. I felt her body pressing against mine and there any distance between us disappeared. I felt our lips meet and I told myself, "Carmen still loves me, still wants me". When she whispered, "Brownie, I missed you, so much", I was relieved. I believed her. I told her I loved her, wanted to marry her,

---

28 Staff, Moviefone. "25 Things You Never Knew About 'An Affair to Remember'" AOL Moviefone. July 10, 2012. Accessed June 13, 2017. https://www.moviefone.com/2012/07/10/an-affair-to-remember-55th-anniversary/.

and take her home with me to America.

But I heard my own words, sounding pathetic. My confidence was shaking, like hers, and she was hesitant and tentative. I had thought she was going to say (what I had dreamed she would always say), at this moment, the moment I had waited for so long. "Yes! Yes! Yes! Brownie, I will marry you".

But instead, she nervously kept shifting her eyes toward the ground. That made me feel she was planting seeds of doubt deeper into my thick head and soft heart. She sheepishly said, "I am going with my Father to see my Grandmother in Spain". I said, "Let's go see her together", but she declined my suggestion. Then, she suggested I meet her in San Sebastian and I agreed.

It was a long train ride over the Pyrenees. A lot of time to think, reflect, hope and pray that this was the right move. The train was packed with people hanging off the back of the train for dear life. Deep in my heart, I knew I was on a journey to hell, but I didn't want to accept it.

When I arrived, I checked into a tiny, cheap hotel, and took a bus to the address she had given me. The streets were narrow and teeming with people. Carmen's grandmother lived on the poor side of town where she was determined not to end up. I found the address, climbed the dim lit stairs and knocked on the door.

Carmen answered and hesitatingly, let me in. Her grandmother, sitting on a stool dressed in black as if she was in mourning, was right out of central casting from a 1940's Bogart and Bacall film noir. From the frustration smoldering on her face, I could tell she wasn't happy and I was not welcome. She was angry (to say the least) that I had come to Spain to take her precious little granddaughter away to America.

I made a faint attempt to be friendly to Grandma until Carmen suggested we "go for a walk". We walked, hand in hand, along a road overlooking the bay of San Sebastian. I knew Christopher Columbus (1451-1506) had set sail for the "new world" from it's deep-water ports. I was making small talk, hoping for bigger things

. . . like marrying the girl of my dreams and raising our family in America.

I didn't know where to begin, didn't know what to say. I asked if she knew about the great Italian explorer from Genoa, Italy, Christopher Columbus. I told her how frightened she must feel about going to America with me. But all she could say with a faint smile was, "Speaking of America, we'll be going to the American Club tomorrow. It's a fancy swim club and I have lots of friends there. Whatever you do, don't call me Carmen, call me, Nancy".

At the American Club, everyone greeted her as 'Nancy'. What happened to Carmen? This was a different Carmen and the guys surrounding her were a different audience consisting of rich boys, in designer clothes, wrap-around sunglasses, subserviently bringing her drinks. She had them in the palm of her hands. I felt like I was back in Newark again, back in the Fabian Swim Club, an exclusive club in the Weequahic section of Newark, where I had gotten into a fist fight after being caught sneaking in.

I had to get out of there. I insisted that we leave. She protested, but I wouldn't take no for an answer. As we stood at her doorway, I wanted more time with her, but she begged off saying she was tired and wanted to go to sleep. She promised to see me "tomorrow" and kissed me goodnight. She told me that her uncle was taking the same bus and would show me the way back to my cheap hotel.

I hopped onto the dirty, crowded, smelly bus, headed back towards my hotel. Carmen's uncle, who was standing next to me, holding on to one of the leather straps hanging from the ceiling of the bus for dear life, was measuring me up and down and then with pity in his eyes, said, "She no good". "You nice boy". "She lie to you". "Go home". "She no love you". "She no for you, go home". "She go out tonight with more boys".

I looked at him as if he was out of his mind . . . at least I was hoping he was. I got off the bus and went up to my room, I fell onto my bed, exhausted, tired of all the doubt beginning to hang heavy on me. I couldn't get to sleep as all I could hear was his words, "She lie to you, go home, she no love you, she no for you, go home, she goes out tonight with more boys" in my head.

I had to see for myself. Throwing my clothes on, I went back out and took the bus back across town to the narrow street where her grandmother lived. It was beginning to get dark as I stepped off the bus. I could hear people laughing, partying in the small bars along the narrow street. I started peering into the clubs and dives hoping not to find her.

But in one of the bars, there she was, bubbly, and beautiful, playing a pinball machine next to a jukebox with a bunch of young guys gathered around her. She was playing her game, giggling and having such a good time with them. With my insides screaming, she didn't see me as I turned and walked away. I had wanted our reunion to be a Hollywood movie. But somebody up there was writing the script and the ending written was not the one I'd hoped for. I was lost as the bus drove me back to my hotel. I fell asleep in my clothes. The feelings I had, inspired the song I wrote years later with my wife, Lisa, for Johnny Mathis called "Gone, Gone, Gone".[29]

I got up the next morning and proceeded to meet her where we'd agreed to meet the night before. She threw her arms around me to give me a hug and kiss. I backed off and told her "Give me my passport and the money I had left with you for safe keeping". She protested, but gave them to me, begging me to tell her why I was so upset. With tears welling up in my eyes I told her, "You know why. I saw you last night at the bar playing pinball with those guys". I heard her begin to cry, "Don't go, Brownie", but I was already gone.

---

29 Johnny Mathis recorded "Gone, Gone, Gone" written by L. Russell Brown and Lisa Hayward, (1972), Columbia Records

It's a mystery I cannot explain

Only clues I got are heartaches and pain

Since she's gone, gone, gone, gone, baby's gone

I wonder, wonder, wonder

Where she's gone, gone, gone, gone, baby's gone

I can't sleep at night, got no appetite

Everything is wrong that used to be right

Since she's gone, gone, gone, gone, baby's gone

I wonder, wonder, wonder

Where she's gone, gone, gone, gone, baby's gone

Ooh, yes, I tried to change her

Tried to re-arrange her personality

Ooh, God I'm paying now

I just cannot seem to face reality

I can't sleep at night, got no appetite

Everything is wrong that used to be right

Since she's gone, gone, gone, gone, baby's gone

I wonder, wonder, wonder

Where she's gone, gone, gone, gone, baby's gone

It's a mystery I cannot explain

Only clues I got are heartaches and pain

Since she's gone, gone, gone, gone, baby's gone

I wonder, wonder, wonder

Where she's gone, gone, gone, gone, baby's gone

Like Tom Hanks in the movie *Forrest Gump*, I walked, walked, and walked struggling for some answers. I found myself on a beautiful Basque hillside overlooking the bay of the glorious northern Spanish city of San

Sebastian. It was beginning to rain, but nothing like the torrent of tears falling from my eyes. I must have cried for half an hour. I pulled myself together, went back to the hotel, got my things, and with just enough money for a ticket, jumped onto the train back to Paris.

I asked to speak to the consulate at the U.S. Embassy in Paris as I was broke and needed to find a way home, as had many before me,

> The United States Embassy in Paris, France was America's first diplomatic mission, and some of our "founding fathers" (Benjamin Franklin, John Adams, Thomas Jefferson and James Madison) were among our first envoys to France . . . The Embassy is located on Avenue Gabriel near the Place de la Concorde, Metro Concorde.[30]

I had a terrible tale to tell. After a short wait, I was ushered into a large room to an embassy rep who pointed me towards another room. I waited there with several other young fools who had similar stories which was that "I'd been out of the army for a short time and I needed help getting back to the states". We had a good laugh at each other's expense.

---

[30] Embassy of the United States, Paris, France, History & Location, http://france.usembassy.gov/embassy_location.html

I'm comin' home, I've done my time

Now I've got to know what is and isn't mine

If you received my letter telling you I'd soon be free

Then you'll know just what to do

If you still want me, if you still want me

Tie a yellow ribbon 'round the ole oak tree

It's been three long years, do you still want me?

If I don't see a ribbon round the ole oak tree

I'll stay on the bus, forget about us, put the blame on me

If I don't see a yellow ribbon 'round the ole oak tree

Bus driver, please look for me

'Cause I couldn't bear to see what I might see

I'm really still in prison and my love, she holds the key

A simple yellow ribbon what's I need to set me free

I wrote and told her please

Tie a yellow ribbon 'round the ole oak tree

It's been three long years, do you still want me?

If I don't see a ribbon round the ole oak tree

I'll stay on the bus, forget about us, put the blame on me

If I don't see a yellow ribbon 'round the ole oak tree

Now the whole damned bus is cheerin'

And I can't believe I see

A hundred yellow ribbons round the ole oak tree.

We had paid our dues and now belonged to an exclusive club called "The Stupidos" (Italian for idiots). It's a universal term probably born out of a moment just like this one. But at least I wasn't alone and after all, how can anyone ever write a song about a broken-hearted fool, unless you've been one. I was coming home. Maybe that's where my inspiration for one of my biggest hits comes from. Thank you, thank you, thank you, Tony Orlando and Dawn.[31]

---

[31] Tony Orlando and Dawn recorded "Tie a Yellow Ribbon Round the Ole Oak Tree", written by Irwin Levine and L. Russell Brown (1973), Bell/Elektra Records

Chapter 12

Lisa

Donny Kirshner, the legendary music publisher, (and another Beth Israel alumni) had a stable of killer songwriters signed to his company, Screen Gems Music. Their success was daunting. I remember a nice little Jewish girl from Brooklyn, a gifted genius, Carole King, and her brilliant lyricist husband, Gerry Goffin, who wrote many classics including "Will You Still Love Me Tomorrow?," "Up on The Roof", and, "The Locomotion".

The ones they didn't write for Kirshner's Music Publisher company were created by his other husband and wife team, Barry Mann and Cynthia Weil who wrote "You've Lost That Lovin' Feeling", "You're My Soul and Inspiration", "On Broadway", "Up Town", "We Gotta' Get Out of This Place", and, "He's So Shy". If Bloodworth and I were to have a career in the music industry, we needed to meet Kirshner or another power broker in the industry like him.

Bloodworth and I wrote songs every day and then pitched them to music publishers like Kirshner and others. We were turned down more often than a cheap motel bed. "This ain't what we're looking for" quickly became our professional career theme song.

Our song demos were shoved back into our hands faster than the rise in the price of the toll into the Lincoln Tunnel. What many music lovers don't understand is it takes years to learn how to write songs (in most cases) and then more months to years, if ever, to get labels and the top recordings artists to license the rights to record them.

Songwriting is a tough business and most who try fail. But Bloodworth and I were determined to make it, so we spent most of our time writing new songs and pitching them to music publishers. However, we still had to pay our bills. After going through the old three days to find a job and three hours to lose it routine many times, providence once again intervened, my pal Johnny Price found me a job driving a taxi and to my surprise, the love of my life, Lisa.

* * * *

I drove to the taxi stand at Broad and Market in the late afternoon as business was slow and I needed a fare. I parked, got out, lit a Lucky Strike, leaned against my cab, took a deep breath, and looked around. I remember the first time I saw her walking across the street towards my taxi, a petite, fantastic looking redhead in a tight pink skirt. Couldn't take my eyes off of her. She walked with an air of confidence, but I saw a little unsteadiness in those high heels. We were kindred spirits. I could feel it. Her smile gave her away, cute, but wary of this gruff, cigarette smoking cab driver staring at her.

She caught my glance and I thought she knew what I was thinking. But she didn't have a clue. I could see it in her eyes, read it in her body language. She was an open book and like me, she'd probably had a rough start in life. Later, I found out Lisa had an abusive father and like me, she was suspicious. She was looking for someone to save her. How could she know it was me? We were meant to be, to save each other. It was our destiny and somehow deep in my heart I knew this was going to be more than just a one-night taxi ride. This was a fare that would last forever.

Subsequently, I would learn that Lisa was born five weeks premature and her mother, a victim of her father's constant physical and mental abuse, fled the hospital and disappeared into the inner city of Philadelphia. Five days later the hospital staff named her LaVerne, after the resident nun who was caring for her. For months, her father refused to take her home and when he finally did, he abused her as he did her mother. Her life was a living hell. When she was sixteen, her father remarried. Her new stepmother seemed so sweet and caring, but after a few months, her father took her and her few belongings to live with an Orthodox Jewish family in the Weequahic section of Newark. Her father seemed to have many Jewish friends, I think he was a closet Jew.

I studied her as she crossed Broad Street and waited for the light to change. She crossed Market Street and headed towards me. She looked me up and down and figuring that I was harmless enough, asked if I was free. Was I free? I was free to go anywhere she wanted to go and do anything she wanted to do. Anything that would get me close enough to get my hands on that pretty little thing in the hot pink skirt was just fine with me.[32]

She jumped in and gave me an address, in the Weequahic section of Newark. I smiled and on the way, I couldn't help staring at her in my rearview mirror. I asked her to turn her head so I could see her from another angle. I knew that bothered her, but I asked for her name and when she said, "Lisa", I knew I had gotten to first base.

To this day, she has no idea why she chose that name. She just made it up on the spot. Lisa, LaVerne, hum, sound familiar as in Carmen, Nancy? I could see she

---
[32] George Strait recorded "I Thought I Heard My Heart Sing", from the album "Love is Everything", written by Bill Kenner and L. Russell Brown, (2016) MCA Records

had been crying and I asked her why. She brushed it aside and asked, "You're a songwriter, aren't you?" I figured she knew my sister, Annette. "You know my sister, Annette?" "Yes", she responded, but she didn't really know her. Lucky guess or maybe providence was just smiling down on us. I asked if we could stop at a diner. I was dying for a cup of coffee.

I wondered if she might want one too. So, I came out with two cups of coffee, but she turned me down. She didn't want any part of me, at least not yet. I drove her to her destination and gave her my phone number, which she reluctantly took and put in her pocketbook. I told her I wasn't going to charge her for the ride. She insisted on paying, but I wouldn't take her money.

I drove back downtown to the Military Park Diner and jumped into a seat next to Paul Abbatemarco (1934-2004), another taxi driver. "Paul, I just met the girl I'm gonna' marry". "You're a 'botchagaloot' Brown, how could you possibly know you're gonna' marry a girl you just met?" Superstar George Strait may provide the answer as he recently recorded my song "I Thought I Heard My Heart Sing."

Well, I do what my heart says do	Well, here I am knocking on your door
And right now it's pointing at you	This old hound wants to talk a little more
Hey girl, you're tugging' on my heart strings	The T.V.A. and the Hoover dam
Well, I've seen everything	Don't turn me on like holding your hand
I thought I heard my heart sing	Well, I've seen everything
I went home flying high	I thought I heard my heart sing
I met the girl of my dreams tonight	Well, I've seen everything
A wild fire, screamin' inside	I thought I heard my heart sing
I know it's real 'cause the heart don't lie	Heart sing

I was hoping for a call, but it didn't come. Weeks went by. Then, one day, out of the blue, the phone rang at my parent's house. I picked it up and heard that whisper like voice that I had heard coming from the back seat of my taxi just a heartbeat ago. She said, "Is Larry there?" I responded, "Lisa?" she said, "How did you know it was me?" I said, "I've been waiting for your call" "Good". "Larry, would you come and pick me up, I need a ride"?

I couldn't wait to get there. I flew out of the house, jumped in my car and was there in no time flat. I opened the door for her and asked where she wanted to go. I found out years after we were married that I had driven to her boyfriend's house that night!

That wasn't the last time she called and asked me for a ride, but I was happy just to be with her. She didn't know it then, but when I was driving her, she was driving me crazy. Those rides led us to our final destination, each other's arms! We began seeing one another every single day, every single night-until we didn't want to be single anymore. Two years later, we were married.

It didn't take us long to start building our own family. I remember the morning we were on our way to the hospital. Lisa was having labor pains and they were coming hard and fast. We gingerly walked down the three flights of stairs to the car and I began to drive her to Saint Michael's Hospital in Newark. We hadn't been driving for five minutes when she begged me to stop at the diner and get her a cup of coffee. I protested but she insisted. She had her coffee and we arrived at the hospital at 7:30 that morning.

I was in the waiting room for over two hours when Dr. Roston finally came out and told me to go home. I was exhausted. I left after he promised me that as soon as they felt she was going to deliver, they would call me. I fell asleep on our red velour couch. The ringing of the phone woke me at 1:45 pm and I was the father of a little girl. Heidi Sara Brown was born on Father's Day, June 19, 1966.

I rushed to the hospital. Lisa had endured a difficult birth and she looked totally spent. The hospital allowed her to be discharged, but decided to keep our baby for observation overnight, as her temperature was unusually high. We were both quite upset about leaving our newborn baby at the hospital. But good sense prevailed and we went back to our tiny third floor apartment and waited to hear from the doctor.

We spent the better part of that week at the hospital hoping Heidi's temperature would abate and we could take her home. After a week, we were not going to let them keep her any longer even though her temperature was still well over one hundred two degrees. Lisa insisted on bringing Heidi home.

The hospital staff told us if anything happened to her, they would not bear any responsibility. Lisa and I had similar beginnings. We were and still are rebels of sorts. People of authority didn't intimidate us then and they don't now. Thank God. We took our baby home. We contacted a pediatrician, Dr. Ingrid Hoffman, who was recommended by a close friend. Our future baby doctor advised us to begin swabbing Heidi down with cool water. We then put her in the bathtub in room temperature water.

Heidi is now in Nashville, Tennessee where she has been teaching art to challenged children. Heidi's high school guidance counselor told her upon graduation that she wasn't "college material". My wife and I realized although she had been a social butterfly in high school, Heidi was as smart as a whip. We decided to enroll her in a private college in Henniker, New Hampshire, where she made the Dean's List.

After six months, she was accepted to Penn State University where she graduated with honors. She then went on to get her teaching degree at Middle Tennessee State University and recently received her master's degree from Boston University. And, the State of Tennessee recently gave its first Humanities Teacher of the Year in Art (for a secondary school teacher) to Heidi!

Dr. Hoffman saved Heidi's life and eight years later saved our second child, Jennifer, when she realized Jen would die if she didn't get immediate treatment. After Jennifer was examined at the Children's Hospital in New York City, it was determined that the tubes connecting her kidneys to her bladder were not long enough. This condition was causing reflux, which led to an infection in Jennifer's intestinal tract.

If it wasn't corrected immediately, it could be fatal.

Dr. McGovern at the Children's Hospital had recently invented a procedure to save his own children from the same condition. He was willing to perform the procedure on Jennifer. The operation took close to seven hours, as they had to disconnect, stretch, and reconnect the tubes in Jenny's stomach.

I had written a book for Jennifer at the hospital to help give her strength and courage for her ensuing operation. It was called "Jenny the Tiger," about a little girl sailing on a stormy sea. The ship was being smashed by the waves and terrible winds, but she never gave up because she was, "Jenny the Tiger." At the end of the story, "Jenny the Tiger" passed through the storm and the sun was shining. It ended with a beautiful sunny sky. The book was filled with my brightly colored Jenny inspired drawings and she still has it to this day.

Jennifer has become a spectacular artist. One of her great accomplishments was a painting of a mural on the walls of St. Jude's Children's Research Hospital in Memphis, Tennessee. This hospital has a rich and blessed history,

> *Danny Thomas was one of 10 children born to Lebanese immigrant parents, Thomas . . . began to help support the family at age 10 by selling newspapers and at 11 he became a candy maker in a burlesque theater, a job he held for seven years . . . When Rose Marie (his wife), was about to give birth to their first child, Margaret (later Marlo), he was torn between his dedication to his work and his responsibility to his wife and their new baby. Desperate, Danny sought relief in prayer. He knelt before the statue of St. Jude, the patron saint of the hopeless causes and begged for a sign . . . and promised to erect a shrine to St. Jude if the saint would show Danny his way in life . . . Mr. Thomas went on to become one of the best-loved entertainers of his time, starring in shows in New York and Chicago, Hollywood movies and in the television series "Make Room for Daddy," which evolved into one of the most successful and honored family comedy shows in television history. Mr. Thomas never forgot his promise to St. Jude. The shrine would be a hospital for needy children, a place where they would be cared for regardless of race, religion or ability to pay.*[33]

She has also painted murals in schools and churches in the Memphis area. She has worked in the ghetto, painting and cleaning up downtrodden neighborhoods. God has a special plan for us all and he needed Jennifer

---
33 St. Jude's Children's Research Hospital, Thomas Family, Danny Thomas, Founder

to survive so she could be an inspiration for so many needy people. I never preached about intolerance to my three daughters. They could see by the people who came to our home, dined at our table, and made music with their father, bigotry was not a part of our psyche, or in our hearts.

Chapter 13

Connecting the Dots

Nineteen sixty-three was a turbulent time in American history. Vietnam, student protests, Kent State, assassinations. America was turning a hard left politically and music was reflecting the change. On any given night, Bob Dylan, Joan Baez, Peter, Paul, and Mary, and even groups like The Byrds, were performing in the bars and coffee houses of Greenwich Village.

Bloodworth and I could feel the excitement building and we wanted to be a part of this new "folk music scene". So, we started playing as the Distant Cousins. We played Kingston Trio songs, "Hang Down your Head Tom Dooley", "Where Have All the Flowers Gone" and we kept playing the Everly Brothers' songs, too. Little did we know that another group somewhere far away was also playing those Everly Brothers' songs.

They were also developing a new sound by combining rhythm and blues (also called R&B) to old traditional country music. The Beatles were coming!

This is a crazy business but success often depends on who you know and who they may know. Johnny Price, my boyhood pal had a friend, Joel Neiman, (a fellow teacher) who was dating Francine Levine whose brother, Irwin, was a successful songwriter. Johnny told me that I had to meet him, so we connected at Levine's parent's house in Irvington, New Jersey.

We hit it off, but he was involved with a couple of other writers and had an exclusive writer's deal with Hal Webman's (d. 2004), publishing company called *We Three Music*. He wasn't about to start writing with an unknown. However, he was kind enough to give me the phone number of Nevel Nader, a middle-aged Lebanese man and a real character, who had already written several hit songs. He had an exclusive songwriter's agreement with Aaron Schroeder's (1926-2009) publishing company. Aaron was a successful songwriter in his own right, who had written several hit songs including, "Wear My Ring Around Your Neck" and "It's Now or Never" for Elvis.

I called Nevel and he invited me to drop by his hotel room. It was a flophouse close to Chess Records, just off of Seventh Avenue. I went up to his room and he answered the door in his underpants. He looked like Lou, from the comedy duo, Abbot and Costello. Sitting bleary eyed on the edge of the bed he said, "play me a couple of your songs".

I took out my guitar and he liked what he heard. Considering that he already had written some hits under his belt including "Mecca", for Gene Pitney and "Punish Her" for recording artist Bobby Vee, I was thinking he could be the connection I needed. That was until he asked me, "Would you mind if I took a leak?" I told him to help himself. He got off the bed, waddled over to the sink about fifteen feet away peed into it. Finishing, he apologized for not having a toilet as he wandered back to the bedside. I shook my head thinking to myself, this guy's gonna' help me? Who's gonna' help him? But I liked this primitive poet, he made me laugh. We decided to meet and try writing a song together.

After we had gotten to know each other a little better, I asked Nevel if he'd be willing to meet my singing partner. He agreed and Raymond and I auditioned for him in his bedroom, or should I say bedroom/bathroom. He was impressed and said with the right material we could be successful.

The three of us began writing together and the story just keeps getting weirder. Nevel moved into a nicer apartment on Eighth Avenue with his friend, Dick Wegryzn who may have been nuttier than he was. Dick Wegryzn (let me emphasize the word "dick") had invented the "stay down zipper" (the zipper that keeps men's pants fly zippers from opening). He made a goodly sum of money selling it, so Nevel and I persuaded "Dicky boy" to invest twenty-five hundred dollars in a demo recording for Bloodworth and me.

We stuck with our name, The Distant Cousins. He hired

Bob Halley, an accomplished arranger, and purchased studio time in one of New York's finest recording studios, Regent Sound. We had the top studio musicians in New York City.

I played lead guitar on the session. Singing the key song on that day, "To Have and To Hold," Raymond and I, with our Everly Brothers' harmony, sounded a lot like the Beatles. Bob Halley, our arranger, liked us and introduced us to Harriet Wasser, Bobby Darin's (1936-1973), publicist. Harriet also knew the legendary hit songwriter/publisher/producer, Bob Crewe. This kind of elaborating networking is at the heart of the business, and, if you don't do it, you'll probably never make in the industry. You never know who knows the next person who can help you get where you want to go.

Bob Crewe had just accomplished something that no one in history had ever done. His new group, Frankie Valli and The Four Seasons, who he produced and wrote songs for, just had three number one records in a row. It was unprecedented. Harriet took our recordings to Crewe. He told her he was going to sign us and release the record on his own, newly formed label, Dynavoice Records. We waited for what seemed like an eternity for the appointment to meet Crewe, but it didn't happen. Months went by and still no call, the story of my life. But it was about to have a new chapter.

Out of the blue, Nevel called us, telling us to go to Bob Crewe's offices at 1841 Broadway, 6th floor, and to be prepared to sign a record deal.[34] We were ushered into his brother Dan's office on the same afternoon about 3pm. He was Bob's right hand man and was going to officiate at the signing. After we signed the agreement (without the advice of counsel, not an unusual practice in 1964), Dan asked us if we would like to meet his brother Bob, to which we both answered, "YES!"

We waited for hours. Finally, Dan escorted us into Bob Crewe's office. I was awestruck. The walls were lined with gold records. Bob Crewe, with his movie star good looks similar to Robert Redford on his best day, stood

---

34 Bob Crewe, pop songwriter and producer for Frankie Valli and others, dies at 83. By Adam Bernstein, Washington Post, http://www.washingtonpost.com/entertainment/music/bob-crewe-pop-songwriter-and-producer-for-frankie-valli-and-others-dies-at-83/2014/09/12/b459cdc4-3a94-11e4-8601-97ba88884ffd_story.html

up from behind his desk, reached out his hand with a dramatic flair and briskly shook our hands. From the second I looked into this brilliant genius's eyes, (one of his companies was named, Genius Inc.), I knew my life was about to change.

After a few minutes of kind words and praise for our work he asked us to sing for him. This was the moment I had been waiting for, dreaming of, working towards since the day I wrote my first song. I had a feeling this had better be good or it might be my ticket back to the taxi stand. We sang and played for all we were worth and he was so excited he asked us to sing another song, and that led to another.

For over an hour we sang and played for this beautiful man. By the time darkness fell over Central Park, Crewe had seen the light, and he asked us if we would like to write songs, full time, for his publishing company, Saturday Music. That would be a YES. I also asked Crewe if our co-writer, Nevel Nader, could be included in the deal as we wanted to keep the peace, and he was.

We were on cloud nine and began writing for his company the following week. The salary was a skimpy fifty bucks a week, but Bob arranged an appointment for us to meet Thea Zavin (1922-2004), the Vice-President of BMI (Broadcast Music Inc.), which is the larger of the three American performing rights societies. The other two are ASCAP (American Society of Composers, Authors, and Publishers), and SESAC which used to mean something, but they now call themselves by their initials.

In the United States, we have three of these companies who collect licenses fee or royalties from companies that use our songs in a public performance such as a live concert, nightclubs, or radio station airplay. As an example, a number one song on pop, country, or rock stations may generate about half a million dollars in revenues, usually split between the songwriter(s) and the music publisher(s).

Thea welcomed me into her office at BMI headquarters on 57th Street. "So, you're the young man my dear friend, the great Bob Crewe, told me about". She paused for a moment and looked at some documents. Then, she shook her head and said, "We already have a Larry Brown writing for BMI". I told her my legal name was Lawrence. She peered down at her papers again and shaking her head said regrettably, "We have a Lawrence Brown, too".

She went on to explain the problems similar names would cause in logging my songs. Thea asked if I had a middle name. "Yes, it's Russell". "That does it". "Would you mind if we called you, L. Russell Brown for logging purposes?" "That's fine with me". At which point she said something that, at that time in my life, was music to my ears "We're going to match the fifty dollars a week Bob Crewe has promised to pay you".

Thea was always one of my favorite people in the industry. I remember the last time I saw her in New York. She was in her late 80s, at a party at BMI Headquarters, and as usual, she had a cigarette lit in both hands! Of course, I went up and thanked her for giving me my name, and as I was leaving, I heard her say, "Larry! Let me know if anybody else in this business needs a name!" What a doll!

Still, one hundred dollars a week was still not enough to support Lisa and me. She would have to continue working at Westinghouse. She got up at six a.m., went to Bloomfield Avenue in Verona, across the street from the nice apartment we had rented, took the bus several miles to work, where she had to wear safety gloves to handle the hot bulbs she was assigned to assemble.

She suffered from burns on her arms because the gloves only went up to her wrists. Lisa believed in me and had an undying faith in our dreams. I was determined to make them all come true. She was my inspiration and she worked her heart out. But when her little belly got too big from the baby we had conceived the first month we were married, she quit her job.

By the spring of 1966, I was making four hundred dollars a week working exclusively for Bob and Dan, better known in the business as the Crewe brothers. Bob was making millions and Dan was his right-hand man. Bob had all the drugs, sex, and rock n' roll money could buy. Rumor had it that he was not only sleeping with a gorgeous six-foot tall Native American model, but also with her muscle-building husband. And neither one of them knew it! One afternoon I walked into Bob's office.

He was ashen faced, shaking: I asked him, "What's wrong, Bob?" He told me the man in the lobby was there to kill him. The muscle builder had finally found out that Crewe was sleeping with his wife. I told Bob, "If you want him to leave, I'll take care of it for you". Bob said, "Go ahead, Larry, please, try, but I doubt it".

On my way, out to the lobby I passed the stock room where I knew they stored a crow bar. I started patting the powerful piece of metal on my hand as I approached Bob's bulked-up, pissed-off lover. I looked him straight in the eye and borrowing Richard Widmark's (1914-2008) sinister smile, I said, "You're gonna' have to get out of here". "Now, understand?" There was a long moment of silence. He measured me. Then thought better of it and walked toward the elevator. I walked back into Bob's office and gave him the good news. Crewe was close to tears thanking me. He hugged me, said he loved me. I loved him too and still do to this day.

I will never forget my favorite Bob Crewe lyric. It was never used in a song. He was producing Lesley Gore (1946-2015) of "It's My Party", and "You Don't Own Me" fame. Her mother and father were so domineering, so controlling of her life that Crewe referred to them as a 'smother' and a 'bother'. Pure genius!

Chapter 14

Tour-de-Force

After three years of writing dozens of 'also ran' songs with Bloodworth, we were booked onto Dick Clark's (1929-2012) national tour as The Distant Cousins. Appearing on Dick Clark's TV show American Bandstand was a huge break for us as it was the most important show for breaking new acts at the time. Clark's show was broadcast Monday through Friday on national TV in the early afternoon out of Philadelphia.

Teenagers getting out of school would zip home to catch the show. It was a great way for all of us to "discover" the newest hits and acts and to learn the newest dance steps. If you haven't seen the show, here's a description.

> *American Bandstand brought rock 'n' roll music into millions of households and showed Americans how to do the latest dance steps. Dick Clark, "America's Oldest Teenager" hosted the series for most of its run. Regular Bandstand segments*

> were "The Spotlight Dance," "Rate-A-Record" and the "American Bandstand" Top 10 Countdown. "The Spotlight Dance" featured 2 or more couples dancing to a softer tune. "Rate-A-Record" had teenage contestants rate and comment on a record played on the show. The "American Bandstand Top Ten" was a countdown of the Top 10 hits of the day.[35]

Bloodworth and I knew this was our first really big break that might launch us into being superstars. We were promoting our charted single, "She Ain't Lovin You No More". As excited as we were, I could not believe what happened as Dick turned to the audience and proclaimed, "And now, The Distant Cousins!" I was standing next to him (Dick Clark), and was so excited.

But, without looking, I raised my guitar so fast it struck him hard on the head! I wanted to die. I thought my career would end right then and there. He glared at me as he rubbed his head, but quickly turned his scowl into that familiar American Bandstand smile. As I would soon learn, like everything else about him that smile came from the heart. Dick Clark was all of that and more, a most elegant, consummate professional. He

---
35 American Bandstand, Overview, TV.com.http://www.tv.com/shows/american-bandstand/

never lost his cool. Without trying, he taught me how to maintain mine. Raymond and I put on a great show that night for him.[36]

The tour was a fascinating experience. I met and became friends with some amazing young, talented artists, who would one day be inducted into the Rock n' Roll Hall of Fame. Among them, a crazy and wild Jeff Beck and a very gifted guitar player, Jimmy Page, whose story goes like this:

> *Jimmy Page grew up in working class West London and took up the guitar at age 13, learning to play mostly by teaching himself. A fan of bluesmen like B.B. King and Buddy Guy, Page played well enough to be hired as a session musician in the mid-Sixties, appearing on tracks by the Who, the Kinks and many others. When Eric Clapton quit the Yardbirds in 1965, Page replaced him. . . Jimmy Page is best known as the fire-slinging riffmaster who helped Led Zeppelin to hard-rock dominance in the 1970s. His work with Zeppelin made him one of rock's most important and influential guitar players, writers, and producers; in 2003, Rolling Stone listed Jimmy Page as number nine on its list of the 100 greatest guitarists of all time.*[37]

---

36 The Distant Cousins recorded "She Ain't Lovin You No More" written by Raymond Bloodworth and L. Russell Brown (1966) Date Records
37 Jimmy Page, Biography, Rolling Stone, http://www.rollingstone.com/music/artists/jimmy-page/biography

Jeff Beck always needed an ample supply of guitars. If he wasn't happy with his performance he would stalk off stage in a rage and smash his 'axe' into smithereens. He was inconsolable, such a perfectionist, so dedicated to his craft. I had never seen anyone like him before. And, who was he?

> Jeff Beck broke into the music scene in 1966 after joining the Yardbirds. Although his stint with the band lasted only 18 months, Beck played on almost all of the group's hits. More importantly, Beck's innovative style heard on classics like "Heart Full of Soul" and "Shapes of Things" helped influence the psychedelic sound of the '60s.[38]

The Dick Clark tour started in Amarillo, Texas. On one of our first days on the bus, Jeff and Jimmy and the other members of the Yardbirds, who dressed in strange old English outfits, with long hair and super high-heeled shoes, began mocking everybody. There were several bands on the bus including Sam the Sham. Jimmy and Jeff laughingly referred to them as, "Sam the Joke". Sam the Sham and the Pharaohs was a one hit, well maybe two hit wonder-

---
38 Jeff Beck, Biography, Jeff Beck Official.com, http://www.jeffbeckofficial.com/biography/

> Sam the Sham stated as a 60s Tex-Mex rock 'n' roll band. Lead singer Domingo "Sam" Samudio formed the group in 1961 in Dallas, Texas, USA . . . Samudio resurrected The Pharaohs in 1963 . . . The band scored their greatest smash hit with the wonderfully raucous "Wooly Bully," which sold over three million copies and stayed on the Billboard Top 40 charts for 18 weeks . . . "Wooly Bully" was named Record of the Year for 1965 by "Billboard" magazine. The bubbly "Li'l Red Riding Hood" likewise did very well; it peaked at #2 on the Billboard pop charts for two weeks straight . . . Sam the Sham and The Pharaohs disbanded in 1967.[39]

The Yardbirds had a put down for just about every American act on the bus. Ok, so now the gloves come off. I was sitting next to my new pal, the late, great soul singer Bobby Hebb (1938-2010).[40] I stood up and yelled something I can't repeat at the top of my lungs, towards the back of the bus, where the Brits had taken up residence. The Yardbirds came flying at me. We laughed and wrestled our way into a great friendship.

The first show was wild. Bobby Hebb was the opening act. He didn't know it then but he was on his way to

---
39 Sam the Sham and the Pharaohs, Biography, IMDB.com, http://www.imdb.com/name/nm1870655/bio
40 "Bobby Hebb, singer of '66 hit 'Sunny,' dies at 72." TODAY.com. August 03, 2010. Accessed March 16, 2017. http://www.today.com/id/38543709/ns/today-today_entertainment/t/bobby-hebb-singer-hit-sunny-dies/#.WMrb1hiZNgg.

becoming a charter member of the "One Hit Wonder Club" also. I stood in the wings wondering, how could anyone sing one fucking song for over half an hour. It was remarkable and nerve wracking. Bloodworth and I were waiting to go on, but Bobby wouldn't come off. He sang the same song over and over and over again. I later learned the true meaning of the words to his classic song.

He was feeling the "sunshine" on his face. Every night, something was holding him up, sustaining him, driving him on. He once confided in me saying "Larry, I wrote "Sunny" for my mom and my father. They're both blind!" He taught me something about the power of a great song. His legion of fans may not have known the hidden meaning behind the words, but they got the message and gave him back a standing ovation. Every night they loved the song, but enough is enough is enough!

He finally crawled off and we stepped out into the spotlight and froze! Bloodworth was stricken with stage-fright.

Hey, she ain't loving you no more

Hey, she ain't loving you no more

Hey, she ain't loving you no more

Hey, she ain't loving you no more

Boy, that girl gave you the shove

Come on loser join the club

Come on losers join the club

Hate to say I told you so

Hate to me say I told you so

She was mine, I ought to know

She ain't loving you no more

She ain't loving you no more

She's been with so many guys

She ain't never satisfied

Hey, she ain't loving you no more

Hey, she ain't loving you no more

She's been with so many guys

She ain't never satisfied

Hey, she ain't loving you no more

Hey, she ain't loving you no more

I can sympathize with you

Idolized her like you do

Idolized her like you do

Ain't no sense to lose your mind

Ain't no sense to lose your mind

Dry your tears and get in line

Dry your tears and get in line

Again boys

Hey, she ain't loving you no more

Hey, she ain't loving you no more

She's been with so many guys

She ain't never satisfied

I was standing motionless; we were like two wax dummies, one step away from twin mental breakdowns. Now I understood how my father must have felt when he tried to make it as a singer. It must have been like a very bad dream that could have gone something like this:

> *The backstage was noisy and busy as a handsome, short, young man dressed to the 9's, swaggered in confidently. As he quickly opened the dressing room door, an old raggedly dressed stage manager yelled, "You'll be great kid". He knew he was the next great thing and tonight he'd be discovered as he closed the door singing out loudly to himself, the hit "Swinging on a Star".*
>
> *He thought he sounded better than Bing Crosby as he danced across the messy dressing room toward a large mirror. He just knew he had more style, playfulness,*

and an intimate romantic control of his voice that would drive the women crazy, just like Sinatra did in the movies. In his mind, Abe Brown, thought the world was about to discover, the greatest singer ever known. Him! Just one more chance to brush his black naturally curly hair, straighten his tie, and prepare himself as he finished the tune loudly and gracefully accepting the cheer of the non-existence fans with his arms opened widely as a smiled into the cracked mirror.

The pre-show hustle of the stage crew and rehearsal of the musicians was silenced by the drop of pen bouncing off the dusty cracked wood floor darkened dressing room. Sitting backwards in an old chair, was the handsome young man with his head nested in the middle of his folded arms over the back of the seat.

He was a pathetically defeated young man as tears streamed down his face from two bloodshot eyes looking into a future of dismal fate. The old raggedly dressed stage manager passed behind him sweeping up the dirt from the dressing room floor. As he turned toward Abe, he continued sweeping in the direction of the broken young man, stopping in front of the chair.

Don't worry about it kid, you're not the first to kill a career over a little stage fright. I've seen it all, some who turn it around later and some who never recover". Popping the broom up and down a few inches off the ground toward the chair, Abe knew that he was in the way. It was time for him to be swept out with the rest of the trash and dirt.

Just as my father had stage fright at his "shot", so did Bloodworth as he freaked and couldn't go on stage. We had no choice, we had to go on. We began to sing as The Yardbirds were watching from the wings. We bombed. Except for The Distant Cousins, the concert was a huge success. The Yardbirds closed the show. We were astounded at how loud they played and yet they were almost drowned out by the screaming throng who didn't want the night to end. I became a diehard fan and the next day they didn't let me down.

We arrived in Oklahoma and Jeff Beck took me aside, "Brown, you need help". "You're comin' with us today". "We're going to the Army and Navy store, you're missing something". "You need a gimmick, a look, something different". And did I get it. I was sporting a beard and mustache. They somehow persuaded me to shave off the left side of my mustache and the right side of my beard. They outfitted me in a hunter's camouflage suit, topped it off with an Australian outback hat and then handed me a giant bullwhip. Beck said' "Snap it as if you're taming the wildest beast in the jungle".

That night, after another prolonged performance from Bobby Hebb, the Distant Cousins took the stage. The animals were waiting. I snapped the whip twice and they went wild! Teenyboppers screaming at me! A wall of sound that snapped me out my fears and woke Raymond out of his coma. He could smell the blood, too. We brought the house down that night and every night after that.

I remember Jeff Beck, Jimmy Page, Keith Relf, Jim McCarty, and Chris Dreja, still hear them carrying on into the night, drinking, laughing. Maybe those old Yardbirds are wondering, "Whatever happened to Larry Brown, that madman of The Disant Cousins?" Cheerio mates, here I am, hey boys, it's me, L. Russell Brown, the co-author of the most recorded American song in history.

****

Bloodworth and I wrote, "C'mon Marianne" on a Wednesday. Crewe played it for Frankie Valli and Bob Gaudio (b. 1942, also of The Four Seasons) on Friday. They recorded it over the weekend with the group. I heard it on Monday, in heavy rotation on every radio station in the "Big Apple".

Crewe had me play my guitar to show the "feel" we were looking for the band to record. On "C'mon Marianne", the opening guitar licks are mine, as we couldn't get the guys in the band to do it the same way, so Crewe just kept mine in the recording. The song was also a big hit for Donny and Marie Osmond in the 1970s and played a pivotal role in the 2005 Broadway show *Jersey Boys*.

New York had once eaten me up and spit me out. "C'mon Marianne" was the "Pick of the Week" on WMCA, WINS, and on the Big Kahoona station, WABC, where the monster DJ himself, Bruce Morrow, better known as *Cousin Brucie*, presided over the fortunes and fate of every recording artist in the western world. [41]

---
41 After Decades on the Dial, Cousin Brucie Falls Victim to a Changing Media World, By Ben

Marianne, Marianne, Marianne, Marianne

Whoa ho ho here I am on my knees again

I'll do anything just to make it right

Say you'll understand, oh I know you can

C'mon Marianne

No matter what the people say, it didn't happen that way

She was a passing fling and not a permanent thing

Say you'll understand, oh I know you can

C'mon Marianne (baby)

C'mon Marianne (baby)

C'mon Marianne (baby)

Say you can understand

My Marianne, Marianne, Marianne, Marianne

Well now your big brown eyes are all full of tears

From the bitterness of my cheatin' years

So I hang my head, wish that I was dead

C'mon Marianne (baby)

C'mon Marianne (baby)

C'mon Marianne (baby)

Say you can understand

My Marianne (baby)

C'mon Marianne (baby)

C'mon Marianne (baby)

Recording "C'mon Marianne" with the Four Seasons was thrilling. When Frankie (Valli) arrived, I could see immediately that although he wasn't the tallest guy in the room, he was by far the biggest. In person, he has a karma that is palpable, bigger than life, and honestly, even greater then when he gives interviews on TV or

Sisario, New York Times,http://www.nytimes.com/2005/06/06/nyregion/06brucie.html?_r=0.

does acting stints. I wish he would have played himself when he did the TV show, "The Sopranos". He would have taught them a few things. He doesn't get all the credit he deserves for the astounding success of The Four Seasons.

Their record sales numbers are daunting and the theater version called the *Jersey Boys* will probably play forever. Yeah, he's got that voice; but Frankie played a significant role in their hits too. It was his idea to change the bands' direction and do a 'jazz' type song which led to "Can't Take My Eyes Off of You" and to create those classic pop hits. Frank's partner of 50 years (on a handshake)! Bob Gaudio was the genius composer of the group.

Frank was always directing traffic. He's sharp as hell, always up on current events, and highly opinionated. Don't get him started on politics, the environment, health care; you name it, he'll fill you in. He's a savvy businessman and always interested in new ideas. He loves learning. Linzer remembers Frankie snooping around Crewe's office the day he was in his writing room working on his follow-up single to his number 1 record, "A Lover's Concerto".

Frankie just walked in on him and asked", Hey, what's up? What are you working on?" Linzer replied "Oh, hi, Frank, uh, nothin'," "Just a chorus to a new song for the Toys." "Oh, yeah, let me hear it". "Really?" "Honestly, Frank, I don't know if it's right for you?" "Good, let me hear it". Linzer sang "Workin' my way back to you babe, with a burning love inside". "Yeah, I'm workin' my . . . "Frankie yelled, "That's mine!" Linzer was surprised". Really, you sure?" "Want to wait till I finish it?" "No, go play it for Bobby". "I want Crewe to hear it as soon as it's done". "I want to rehearse it with the group next week".

Go argue with that. Frank Castelluccio, the tough Jersey boy, who always knew a hit song when he heard it. He could hear it from a mile away or standing behind Bob Gaudio, sitting at the piano, locked into the groove of "Sherry", "Big Girl's Don't Cry", and "Walk Like a Man." And yet when it came time to record "C'mon Marianne", it was Bob Gaudio who told me he needed me to play on the record.

He said, "I need you to give the band the feel you got when you wrote it, Larry". "Play it just like you wrote it". I protested to Gaudio who I hardly knew at the time. "You added a key change and I can't put it in the modulated key". Gaudio said "Don't worry, we'll turn your mike off before the key change". It was an incredible thrill to count off a record that would become such a classic.

Chapter 15

Knock Three Times

Nineteen sixty-seven had proven to be a turning point in my career with two million best sellers in three months and with several chart hits during the next few years. Lisa and I were starting to believe I could actually make a good living at this. We were able to buy our own home in Clark, NJ, a small ranch, but it had a beautiful backyard where I put up swings for our two daughters. The neighborhood was nicer than anything we had ever been able to afford.

I started to take the bus into town for writing sessions and that's how I met my next co-songwriting partner. Irwin Levine (1938-1997) and I began running into each other riding the 107 Bus into the city. We soon became great friends. We went to the track, played poker, and dined out together. Irwin was a gem, like the gem of his first two million selling song, "Who Wants to Buy This

Diamond Ring" recorded by Gary Lewis, whose father is the very famous comedian and actor Jerry Lewis . . . who was born in the same Beth Israel Hospital in New Jersey as was I.[42]

Levine also wrote "Black Pearl" recorded by Sonny Charles and the Checkmates. He co-wrote it with Toni Wine and Phil Spector. Knowing Irwin, I'm certain he would have been terribly upset to learn that his old writing partner, Phil Spector (also known for the Wall of Sound), whose work was always considered to be ahead of its time, is now doing time for MURDER!

> Phil Spector was born in New York City on December 26, 1940. Spector got his first hit song while still in high school with a group called The Teddy Bears. Spector went on to write and produce multiple number one songs in the US and UK, also developing the "Wall of Sound" technique . . . Spector produced the Beatles last album "Let It Be", and John Lennon's "Imagine". In 2009, Spector was convicted of the murder of Lana Clarkson, and received a 19-year prison sentence.[43]

Levine was self-taught about most things in this life,

---
42 Gary Lewis And the Playboys, by Gary James, www.classicbands.com, http://www.classicbands.com/garylewis.html
43 Phil Spector Biography, Bio, http://www.biography.com/people/phil-spector-9489973

music included. As a kid, he kept changing schools, probably because he was a constant daydreamer and had very little or no interest in what the teachers were attempting to teach him.[44] Just like I'd been when I was in school. Radio was his teacher. He was a major doo-wop fan and was enamored with R&B 'cause, like him, it had soul. Ironically, he was introduced to the music of black people by a white man who performed in black face, the famous Mr. Al Jolson (1886-1950).

He was Irwin's hero. He could do a mean Jolson at the drop of a hat. In addition, he was connected to Luther Dixon (1931-2009), who was one of Tin Pan Alley's dynamic R&B writer/producers of his day. Irwin was mesmerized by Luther and his songs. The Shirelles were one of the many artists Luther Dixon wrote and produced. Irwin's song, "Our Love's Becoming a Thing of The Past", was produced by Luther and was a popular hit of the day. Levine could write lyrics and music on the bus to New York City. One day he told me he wrote 90 percent of the song "The Diamond Ring"

---

44 Irwin Levine, 58; Wrote 'Yellow Ribbon,' Obituary, the New York Times, https://www.google.com/?client=safari&channel=mac_bm#channel=mac_bm&q=irwin+levine+obituary

by himself riding the bus in.

Luther Dixon was responsible for dozens of pop classics in the 1950s and 60s and helped shape the classic "girl group" sound with the Shirelles . . . His song "Sixteen Candles", co-written with Allyson Khent, was recorded by the Crests and reached No 2 in the US charts in 1959. He produced the hits "Will You Love Me Tomorrow? and "Baby It's You". He also co-wrote "Soldier Boy", "Mama Said", "Boys", "Tonight's the Night" and "Baby It's You". (For the last of these Dixon went under the pseudonym Barney Williams when writing with Burt Bacharach and Hal David).[45]

Irwin Levine was about as shy as Mister Universe at a nudist camp. He was also a great song plugger (a person who gets new songs to artists and labels). Whenever we played one of our new tunes for anyone, he sang it with all his heart and soul! His first chart record was by the great Tom Jones, "Little Lonely One" which was a Levine lyric set to a classic Italian melody. My dear

---

45 Luther Dixon obituary, He wrote dozens of hits in the 50s and 60s by Garth Cartwright. The Guardian, http://www.theguardian.com/music/2009/nov/11/luther-dixon-obituary.

golfing pal, Peter Sullivan, Tom's producer, heard it and Irwin was on his way! Toni Wine and Phil Specter, unlike Irwin's earlier contributions, co-wrote "Black Pearl" making major contributions.

One night, Hank Medress (1938-2007), Irwin, and I were at the YMCA on the Upper West Side to play basketball. Medress had started singing as a member of the Linc-Tones, a vocal group that also included a teenage Neil Sedaka. He formed the Tokens and through hustling found the song "The Lion Sleeps Tonight". We walked through the gym where people were working out on punching bags. A young man in his early 20's was punching furiously on a speed bag. Irwin walked up to the guy and asked if he could hit the bag a few times, which he did. A young man-six foot two, with a build like Charles Atlas, who was standing by, asked Irwin if he wanted to put the gloves on for a little sparring session.

Until that moment, I had never seen Levine box. I didn't even know he could box. He put the gloves on and approached the much taller and younger man. He made a few feints and jabs and instantly the other guy dropped his hands and said, "I don't fight with professionals!" I later found out that Benny Levine, Irwin's father, was a champion boxer from the '30s, and he'd taught Irwin how to box and had taught him well. Although Irwin couldn't hurt a fly, he could have been a contender. The strange thing is that our adventure lead to another great song, this one for another guy who was at the gym that night, Tony Orlando.

Irwin and I were in Medress and David Appell's (Tony Orlando's producer's)[46] office when Hank played me a new recording that Irwin and a superbly talented young female songwriter, Toni Wine, had written. The song was "Candida". Hank wanted my opinion of the record. I told him it couldn't miss. It didn't. At that moment, it was moving up the charts. It was number seventy with a bullet (having a number on the charts with a 'bullet' signifies that sales and airplay are surging). "Candida" became Dawn's first top-five record.

---
46 Dave Appell, Songwriter for Chubby Checker, Dies at 92. The Hollywood Reporter, by Mike Barnes, http://www.hollywoodreporter.com/news/dave-appell-dead-chubby-checker-750811

Before Irwin and I left, Irwin told Hank that Toni Wine had moved to Muscle Shoals, Alabama and was going to marry Chips Moman, Elvis Presley's producer. At that moment, that fateful moment, Hank turned to me and said, "Brown, we're going to need a follow-up for this record, why don't you and Levine write one for me?"

I followed Irwin home that night. He and his wife Sheila lived in a condo in Livingston, New Jersey, directly across from Saint Barnabas Hospital. I didn't have my guitar with me, so I sat down at Irwin's baby grand. I had never written a song on the piano in my life. I could only play in the key of C, but as it turned out, C would be good enough. We discussed writing a Drifter's style song. Irwin remarked that Tony's voice had always reminded him of the great Ben E. King. He said, "Let's write something like "Up on the Roof", which was inspiration enough.

We sat at the piano until Irwin turned to me and asked, "What was it like growing up in the Seth Boyden housing projects?" I told him there were six families in the building. We all had to share one phone. We had heating pipes that ran throughout the building. When someone (who didn't have a telephone) got a call, someone would bang on the heating pipes a certain number of times to let them know the call was for them. This struck a chord in Irwin and he turned to me with that big shit eatin' grin on his lovable, Pancho Villa look-a-like face, and said, "I've got it". "Let's write a song called, 'Knock Three Times'!"

I started a groove. He stopped me and handing me a legal pad and pencil said, "Write this down. Hey girl what you doin' down there, dancin' alone, every night, while I live right above you" I began playing and instantly matched his words with my melody. In a heartbeat, we knew something that millions of record buyers would soon find out. We were magic together. Our songs wrote themselves. We laughed till we cried, jumping for joy as we finished each new little born baby (song we'd written) of ours. And that's not the only great title

Irwin gave us.

We finished "Knock Three Times" and sang it several times, over and over again in disbelief. Could it be that it was as good as we thought? Well, almost. Irwin excused himself saying, "Brown. I've got to go to the bathroom bad!" I said, "Ok, so, go!" I sat at the piano and an idea hit me! I remembered an old Irish drinking song that I had heard back in the early fifties on WNEW, "The Boom, Boom, Boom." The second time they play the chorus, instead of singing, "You'll never get rid of the boom, boom, boom", they beat the drums, boom, boom, boom!

I called out to Irwin, who I was sure by now must have drowned, "I got it, Irwin, let's sing the chorus knock three times and then the next time, let's do what they did in the Irish drinking song "The Tainy" by the Irish Rovers, "Boom, Boom, Boom. We'll let the drums replace it the second time. The same thing with twice on the pipes. Sing it once and then play it on a pipe the second time.

I kept on yelling, "Veene!" "Hurry up and get out here, I got something great!" Finally! He surfaced and I was so excited I couldn't catch my breath, to which he inquired, "What is it already?" I showed him the idea and he freaked out! "I love it. It's a monster hit. Let's play it for Hank in the morning".

We met at Hank's office the next day and sang it for him. He went ballistic. "This is going to be Dawn's next single", convincing Orlando to lend his voice to "Knock Three Times" was a direct violation of Orlando's record company job. By doing that, Medress unwittingly launched the career of one of the most successful pop acts of the '70s, Tony Orlando and Dawn. "Knock Three Times" rocketed up the charts and became a ten million seller in less than three months.[47]

It was reported that it was selling one hundred thousand copies a day, for ten straight days in New York City alone! We were on top of the world and wrote every spare minute of every day looking for it. Success

---

47 Tony Orlando and Dawn recorded "Knock Three Times" written by Irwin Levine and L. Russell Brown, (1973) Bell Records

in the music industry usually leads to problems with money and copyrights.

Crewe owned the publishing rights to all of my songs, but with his expensive habits and extravagant lifestyle he was going broke. He needed money, fast. Irwin was with Five Arts, a management company that was owned and operated by Stanley Polley (1922-2009). They wanted me to sign with them too. I liked Stan Polley as he reminded me of one of my favorite TV personalities, Sgt. Bilko, a fast-talking, lovable con artist. I signed with Five Arts and Stanley negotiated me out of my contract with Crewe and into another one with Wes Farrell (1940-1996):

> *Farrell, was a music executive and songwriter whose four-decade career included the hit pop song "Hang on Sloopy" and the music for the television series "The Partridge Family"...Farrell signed Neil Diamond to his first publishing deal and produced music for the Cowsills, the Everly Brothers and Wayne Newton . . . Farrell was also the chief executive and president of Music Entertainment Group, an umbrella for several music organizations, including one of the country's largest Christian music companies, the Benson Music Group.*[48]

---

48 Wes Farrell, 56, Pop Songwriter Who Created 60's and 70's Hits by Neil Strauss. The New

Wes was a dynamic, chain smoking (the chain that linked to the cancer that took him at such a very young age), record producer/music publisher. Irwin had previously signed an exclusive songwriting contract with him. Now, to conclude my deal, Crewe sold Wes his 50% ownership share of the publishing rights to "Knock Three Times" for $50,000. Wes Farrell asked Irwin and me to come up with a hit song for David Cassidy, the star of the hit TV series, The Partridge Family. So, we wrote, "I Woke Up in Love This Morning", our second RIAA certified million selling single, that reached the top of the charts in 1971.[49]

Six months later, I was out of my contract with Wes Farrell and Irwin was free as well. Tony Orlando decided that with the success of "Candida" and "Knock Three Times" under his belt, he could leave his executive position with April Blackwood Music and devote himself full time to being the lead singer of Dawn, soon to be billed as Dawn, featuring Tony Orlando.

York Times, http://www.nytimes.com/1996/03/02/arts/wes-farrell-56-pop-songwriter-who-created-60-s-and-70-s-hits.html.
49 The Partridge Family recorded "I Woke Up in Love This Morning" from the album Sound Magazine, written by Irwin Levine and L. Russell Brown, (1971), Columbia Records

Hey girl what ya doin' down there

Dancin' alone every night while I live right above you?

I can hear the music playin'

I can feel your body swayin'

One floor below me you don't even know me

I love you

Oh, my darling

Knock three times on the ceiling if you want me

Twice on the pipe if the answer is no

Oh, my sweetness

Means you'll meet me in the hallway

Mmm, twice on the pipe means you ain't gonna show

If you look out your window tonight

Pull in the string with the note that's attached to my heart

Read how many times I saw you

How in my silence I adored you

And only in my dreams did that wall between us come apart

Oh, my darling

Knock three times on the ceiling if you want me

Twice on the pipe if the answer is no

Oh, my sweetness

Means you'll meet me in the hallway

Twice on the pipe means you ain't gonna show

Read how many times I saw you

How in my silence I adored you

And only in my dreams did that wall between us come apart

Oh, my darling

Knock three times on the ceiling if you want me

Twice on the pipe if the answer is no

Oh, my sweetness

Means you'll meet me in the hallway

Mmm, twice on the pipe means you ain't gonna show

But after three straight bomb records, Tony phoned me

and asked if Irwin and I could meet with him for lunch.

He told us that as a consequence of his investment in the group, he was in debt and needed a hit desperately. Over souvlaki, we promised him we would try to come up with another hit.

Last night, I turned out the light,

lay down and thought about you.

I thought about the way that it could be.

Two o'clock, here I am still

Wond'rin' about you.

So, I closed my eyes and dreamed you here to me.

And I woke up in love this mornin'.

I woke up in love this mornin'.

Went to sleep with you on my mind.

I woke up in love this mornin'.

I woke up in love this mornin'.

Went to sleep with you on my mind.

Hello girl, yes, its five o'clock,

I know, but you just listen.

There's something that I've got to let you know.

This is you, this pillow that I'm hugging and I'm kissing.

And one more thing before I let you go.

And I woke up in love this mornin'.

I woke up in love this mornin'.

Went to sleep with you on my mind.

I woke up in love this mornin'.

I woke up in love this mornin'.

Went to sleep with you on my mind.

Do dreams come true?

Well, if they do,

I'll have you not for just a night,

but for my whole life through.

Oh, I woke up in love this mornin'.

I woke up in love this mornin'.

Went to sleep with you on my mind.

I woke up in love this mornin'.

Oh, I woke up in love this mornin'

(Photo by Travis Howard)

Chapter 16

Yellow Ribbon

We wrote every day, so we weren't thinking of Tony when we wrote "Yellow Ribbon". At that point, it was no more than the song written after "Under the Poet's Tree" and the song written before "Beauty Lies in The Eyes of The Beholder". Although its real title is "Tie A Yellow Ribbon Round the Ole Oak Tree", we just starting referring to it as "Yellow Ribbon".

The song was based on a story I had read about a soldier headed home from the Civil War. He wrote to his beloved that if he was still welcome, she should tie a yellow handkerchief around the big oak tree near their town. Levine suggested we change the handkerchief to a yellow ribbon because we blow our noses in handkerchiefs and they are disgusting.

It was nothing more, nothing less. Another song in our

repertoire, another potentially forgotten work, still on a dusty shelf or tucked away in a drawer that no one ever heard or cared about. How many songs suffer this fate? Without someone stepping in or as in our case, two insane writers who wouldn't take no for an answer? Irwin handed me my guitar. "I got it already-check this out". "I'm comin' home, I'm comin' home and I don't really want to be alone. If you received my letter telling you I'd soon be free, then you'll know just what to do if you still want me, if you still want me, tie a yellow ribbon round the old oak tree, it's been three long years do you still want me, if I don't see a ribbon round the old oak tree, I'll stay on the bus, forget about us, put the blame on me, if I don't see a yellow ribbon round the old oak tree".

Sounds good! "I have the second verse, Brown, write the first verse and chorus on the pad, hurry. Brown, change the spelling of 'old' oak tree to 'ole' oak tree, it looks more authentic. Now write this down. Bus driver please look for me. Cause I couldn't bear to see what

I might see. I'm really still in prison and my love she holds the key, a simple yellow ribbon's, what I need to set me free. I wrote and told her please".

We decided to change the first verse. Levin yelled, "Browser, change the first verse now to I'm coming home I've done my time and I've got to know what is and isn't mine". Levine hit on an ending for the song. "Ok, Brown, I got the ending", he said as he told me, "Put the tape machine on record and start singing the song. After the second chorus, you let me sing the ending, you're gonna' love it".

We knew we had created something different. Something very special, with far more potential than our other 'babies'. We had crafted it with the Beatles' music in mind, so it was no accident that Ringo Starr was our first choice to sing it. We took it to 'Mr. Doubting Thomas' a/k/a, Al Steckler, the A&R Director at Apple Records, the Beatle's record company.

Artist and Repertoire (A&R) is the department at most labels who act as talent scouts, looking for new acts and songs to sign at the label, and often includes artist development training acts to write and become public personalities.

After hearing one verse and one chorus of "Yellow Ribbon" Steckler put his hand on the fret of my guitar, deadening the strings. "Boys, this is embarrassing. You've had hits. This could give you a bad name. A stupid song about a ribbon and a tree; come back when you have something good to play me". We didn't know it at the time, but 'Yellow Ribbon' was joining an exclusive club that included some of the greatest songs of all time, unyielding rejection.

Songs including "Somewhere Over the Rainbow", which almost didn't make it into "The Wizard of Oz", and "You Light Up My Life" were turned down by virtually every record company in the business (and later went on to win a Grammy for Song of the Year). They had faced the same insane problem. All of Meatloaf's songs, which made him famous, were initially rejected by the RCA brass who wanted Meat, but not, Jim Steiman's songs. By the way, he was later inducted into the songwriter's Hall of Fame, mostly based on the songs the label "brass" had rejected.

The brick walls songwriters face every day are formidable. But on occasion, like Joshua, we break them down. As Irwin and I waited for the elevator to reach the ground floor, our determination was unwavering. We knew we weren't going down, we were moving on. We would find someone who knew better. Someone with vision, who could hear a hit. Someone with 'platinum ears', someone like our old buddy, Hank Medress.

Remember, Hank was already a highly successful songwriter, producer and had major hits on his resume. He was born and raised in Brooklyn and along with his high school classmate, Neil Sedaka, they formed the singing group, The Linc-Tones. The legendary Sedaka went on to establish a solo career and Hank soon formed another group, The Tokens. "The Lion Sleeps Tonight", their signature song, went to number one in 1961 and Hank was on his way. He soon established himself as an artful, crafty record producer with such classic hits as, "He's So Fine", and "Sweet Talkin' Guy", by the Chiffons.[50]

As often happens in the music business, Hank could not read or write a note of music but had the gift of being able to hear potential hit songs. He could spot a hit a mile away. He was a dynamo. His 'Ben Franklin', 'coke bottle-thick', eyeglasses were his trademark. His eyes shifting constantly, searching for the answers, the right groove, the hidden sound that he would find and the magic that would result in another huge hit.

Irwin and I respected his opinion more than anyone. We called and asked if we could come to his office and play him our new song. We had been striking out for over nine months. We were desperate and although Tony Orlando had never crossed our minds for the song, something told us to play it for Hank. He was always such a positive force. When he entered the recording studio, he filled the room with his enthusiasm and de-

---

50 Hank Medress Biography, Billboard, http://www.billboard.com/artist/1492875/hank-medress/biography

termination. When he left, he took with him some of the greatest memories in recorded history, like the day he left with a copy of "Tie A Yellow Ribbon Round the Ole Oak Tree".

I will never forget the day we played it for him. We sang our hearts out; "Now the whole damn bus is cheering . . ." I glanced over at him to see if he was listening, getting it. He was stoic, contemplating. "And I can't believe I see". He jumped up as if struck by lightning before we could finish the last line. "Smash! A fucking stone hit! I love it. Love it. LOVE IT!" Hank scheduled a meeting with Tony for the next day, telling him that Irwin and I had written a great song for him. He sent Tony and I into the other room and told me to play it for Tony.

Tony surprised me by saying "You should record it, Larry. I like the way you sing it and besides it sounds like a country song". Tony wasn't into it! He was confused. He was going to walk away.

I'm comin' home, I've done my time

Now I've got to know what is and isn't mine

If you received my letter telling you I'd soon be free

Then you'll know just what to do

If you still want me, if you still want me

Tie a yellow ribbon 'round the ole oak tree

It's been three long years, do you still want me?

If I don't see a ribbon round the ole oak tree

I'll stay on the bus, forget about us, put the blame on me

If I don't see a yellow ribbon 'round the ole oak tree

Bus driver, please look for me

'Cause I couldn't bear to see what I might see

I'm really still in prison and my love, she holds the key

A simple yellow ribbon's what's I need to set me free

I wrote and told her please

Tie a yellow ribbon 'round the ole oak tree

It's been three long years do you still want me?

If I don't see a ribbon round the ole oak tree

I'll stay on the bus, forget about us, put the blame on me

If I don't see a yellow ribbon 'round the ole oak tree

Now the whole damned bus is cheerin'

And I can't believe I see

A hundred yellow ribbons round the ole oak tree

I'm comin' home.

I couldn't let him. "Think of it as a Bobby Darin tune, like the Darin classic, "Eighteen Yellow Roses", and then put Bobby Darin's head on," was my suggestion.

He was still skeptical, but he knew that Hank believed it was right for him and he believed in Hank. The rest is history and now he's condemned, closes every show, every performance for the past four decades with "Tie A Yellow Ribbon Round the Ole Oak Tree!"

Hank recorded two songs on Dawn's next session, "Yellow Ribbon" and "You're A Lady". Deciding that the next single for Tony, Thelma, and Joyce would be, "You're A Lady", (a left field hit in England for the singer/songwriter, Peter Skellern), Hank proved he wasn't perfect. And the writer Peter Skellern's dream of becoming a success in the US was kaput, finito, gonzo, over. Henry made another mistake. He let Irwin and me hear a finished copy of "Yellow Ribbon" before it was scheduled to be released. We knew how strong a record it was.[51]

Later, over at Levine's house, Hank called us. He told Irwin that he was not going to release "Tie a Yellow Ribbon Round the Ole Oak Tree" as Tony's next single

---

51 Tony Orlando and Dawn recorded "Tie a Yellow Ribbon Round the ole Oak Tree" written by Irwin Levine and L. Russell Brown, (1974) Bell Records

unless we gave him the publishing rights to the song. I had been tipped off by our 'saintly' manager, Stan Polley that Hank was going to try this maneuver and he confided in me that Medress was only bluffing. But Stanley wasn't; he wanted Hank out of the picture so he could begin laying the groundwork for his own plans to steal the publishing rights to 'Ribbon'.

I said "Veen, give me the phone". Irwin was frightened, petrified that I would sabotage our chances for a much needed, desperately needed hit. "Hank, this is Brown, burn the tapes!" Irwin was aghast as I slammed the phone down. I turned to a visibly shaken Irwin Levine, lighting his twentieth Marlboro of the day. His green fingers were trembling, but somehow, I knew at that moment the green would soon be in both of our hands. "Trust me on this one, Veen. He's bluffing, I'm certain of it".

My wife and I had just purchased Charlie Calello's home which was a major upwards move for us. But I knew that Medress was bluffing and the royalties would soon be coming in. Calello, by the way, is the brilliant producer and arranger who is also from Newark:

> ... Calello has had over 100 Billboard chart records, 38 of which have been top 10. ... Calello became a member of Frankie Valli's group The Four Lovers. In 1962, when the group was transformed into The Four Seasons, he became the newly-rechristened group's arranger. From 1962 to 1965 Calello arranged 21 of their 24 Billboard chart records. ... He arranged Frank Sinatra's Watertown album and the classic song by Neil Diamond, "Sweet Caroline". He has worked with such diverse artists as Shirley Ellis, The Toys, Lou Christie, Al Kooper, Nancy Sinatra, Roberto Carlos, Bruce Springsteen, Barbra Streisand, Engelbert Humperdinck, Glen Campbell, Janis Ian, Barry Manilow, Juice Newton, and many others.[52]

Hank was bluffing and released the recording. Lisa was expecting our third baby and I told her "If this 'Yellow Ribbon' record is not a hit, we're out of this house in six months!" I remember hearing it for the first time on the radio. We were driving out of the Lincoln Tunnel, up the corkscrew that leads onto the New Jersey Turnpike. We knew the record had been released and we were anxiously twisting the dials hoping to catch a

---

52 "Charlie." Charles calello. Accessed July 18, 2017. https://www.linkedin.com/in/charles-calello-52a1b429.

station that might be playing it.

We got WKBW out of Buffalo, New York, a 50-thousand-watt clear channel station, which had the power to reach listeners for hundreds of miles. It sounded unbelievable. The disc jockey came on and pleaded with all those listening, "Please, stop calling the station requesting this song, because you're burning out our switchboard!" Up until this moment our past hit songs were just rescue savers. They would pay the bills for a while, buy us a little more time to try again.

But we were never secure in our minds. There was always that underlying threat of the failure to come up with the next hit song to pay the rent. The thought of our recent hits being our last, always hung over our and most songwriter's heads. But on that day, in that old car, that beat up Barracuda, we heard our life changing song and Levine and I both knew it.

It changed our identity. I was no longer going to be L. Russell Brown, the promising up and coming songwriter from Newark who wrote, "What was the name of that hit again, Larry?" Irwin was no longer going to be remembered as the kid from Irvington who became a songwriter and wrote some hits in the sixties. We would now forever be known as Levine/Brown, the songwriters who wrote, "Tie A Yellow Ribbon 'Round the Ole' Oak Tree". The most successful song in the history of American pop music. There is no feeling like it on earth. That year, 1973, Irwin and I were nominated for a Grammy for Best Song of the Year. With Lisa, proudly on my arm and Sheila, ecstatic and proud on Levine's, we flew out to California for the ceremonies. Our song had been played more than any other song that year. We had sold more than ten million records.

The Vietnam War was finally over and yellow ribbons were everywhere. Our song had been adopted as a symbol to celebrate the return of our troops. The night of the ceremonies, I sat next to Irwin. He was certain that we would win. I knew better. Two days before, being fitted for my tux at Mr. Guy, in Beverly Hills, a swank men's shop, I was introduced to Burt Bacharach. He told me,

"Larry, If I couldn't win with "Raindrops Keep Falling on My Head", you can't win with "Tie A Yellow Ribbon". The music business wants to award songs they think are hip, cool. I had no shot and neither do you".

"Killing Me Softly" was all that and more. It won the Grammy. It was a great song, a classic. But it wasn't as popular as "Yellow Ribbon". Later that year, at the BMI Awards dinner I ran into Charlie Fox, one of the writers of "Killing Me Softly". I lamented to him, "Charlie, I won BMI's (Broadcast Music Inc.), Most Performed Song of the Year, and The First American Music Awards Song of the Year. But you beat me out for the Grammy and I really wanted to win it". He looked at me with a wry smile. "Larry, I'll give you the publishing rights to "Killing Me Softly", and any other song in my catalog in exchange for "Yellow Ribbon". I said, "No way, Charlie". He looked at me, smiled and said, "Then go back to your seat and sit down". Ya gotta' love the guy. To this day, he's still one of my favorite people.

And so that night, Irwin and I had dreamed would be

'our night', we heard "and the Grammy goes to, 'Killing Me Softly', songwriters Norman Gimble and Charles Fox!" The applause drowned out as Irwin jumped to his feet in a rage shouting, "Fuck you, mother fucker!" I hid my face in my hands as Levine, with his world now crushed, got up and stormed out of the building. Lisa and I were numb. Sheila was devastated. He was so sure, so certain that this was our night. But it turned out to be his worst nightmare.

I was disappointed but my heart broke for Irwin. He was angry at me for not feeling as angry as him. He yelled at me on the plane ride home. Before we landed, he asked if he could trade seats with Lisa for a minute. He sat down next to me, put his arm around me and with glazed eyes, told me that he loved me. He was sorry for upsetting me. We laughed and it was over.

Creating songs is collaborating with the angels. Two people become one. They can hear each other's thoughts, feel each other's emotions, and cry tears of joy knowing when it's right, fighting past complacency, mediocrity, when it's almost right, almost there, no not yet, dig deeper to find the right rhythm, the sublime rhyme. Then, in a moment, you can only feel you're at the end of the race, crossing the finish line, in first place! And it all comes together when you hear it for the first time on the radio and then a calm feeling settles over you. It's orgasmic!

Chapter 17

The Money Sharks

For the first time in my life, I was uncomfortable with the feeling of being comfortable while having nothing. Something had to be wrong. Irwin and I had just scored the two biggest hit singles of all time and except for the gold records on our walls, we had very little money to show for it. I was beginning to see how ludicrous those gold records were. I started to understand how awards often come from the people who are profiting from your efforts. Awards are meant to inspire you to write more, produce more, but more for whom? We were about to find out.

In the entertainment business, when the royalties start pouring in, the sharks smell blood in the water. Stanley Polley, along with Terrence Harvey Junior, a former NYC police lieutenant, who had somehow finagled a law degree, had quite a scam going. Everyone who signed a management contract with Five Arts assigned their collective royalty rights to the company. One of the biggest mistakes successful creative people in the industry make is trusting the "suits" to take care of the money.

Big mistake! Polley sold everyone on the idea that all revenues would be consolidated and everyone would share equally in the ownership of the company. His theory, as he explained it, was that every artist has periods when they cool off and during that time, the successful members would help support them. We were his naïve little lambs being led to the slaughter. He controlled the money. Knowing how children are afraid of the dark, he kept us there. When we needed money, he lent us just enough to need more. And more often than not we did.

How Stanley Polley broke into the business is a familiar story of networking in the entertainment business. He got his break after meeting the teen idol, Lugee Alfredo Giovanni Sacco, better known as "Lou Christie", who was really from outside of Pittsburg, PA.⁵³ Christie, in the late 1960s, was a leading singer songwriter, who would go on to perform with The Rolling Stones, The Who, The Supremes, Neil Diamond, and my hero, Little Richard.

> *Polley served in the U.S. Army before beginning his managerial career in New York's garment industry . . . He began artist management after he met (Lou) Christie in the mid-1960s. It was through his association with Christie that he met and began working with other artists in the New York and Los Angeles entertainment industry. He started Five Arts Management around 1968 and in 1970, formed Badfinger Enterprises, Inc, for the British rock group Badfinger.*⁵⁴

Irwin and I could no longer afford to ignore the royalties that were owed to us. Irwin was an innocent man-child, so brilliant and eloquent, so adapt at writing hit songs, yet hopelessly trapped in his fantasy world of writing songs in that sandbox of his mind. I knew I was on my own. I had a sense of urgency that this was going to be my last chance at reaching the holy grail of finan-

---
53 LOU CHRISTIE BIOGRAPHY. Accessed June 24, 2017. http://www.lou-christie.com/bio.html.
54 Stanly Polley, biography, The World Public Library, http://netlibrary.net/Article.aspx?ArticleId=0002576839&Title=Stan%20Polley.

cial security for me and Lisa and our children. Polley had us right where he wanted us, two lovable clowns at his beck and call.

I had to get serious with this vulture, right now! He was raising the stakes. He wanted more, he wanted everything! I had to stand up for my rights, my family, and I didn't mind helping Irwin at the same time. I didn't need a formal education in business and finance to know that nothing was adding up.

I had to figure out what was going on and quickly before it was too late. I had to focus on the business and stop thinking about writing any more fucking songs. "Don't fuck this up, you moron", I kept telling myself. Polley always used to tell us, "Boys, when nothing makes sense, it all makes sense". Yeah, right Polley, dollars and cents in your pocket! Why didn't I get it sooner?

Was it because I was still looking for the nurturing father figure I never had? Had he sensed that about me from the beginning and all the other wayward children he pretended to care about? I had met guys like him before on the streets of Hawthorne Avenue in Newark, when I was ten years old. He was just another cheap hood in a sharkskin silk suit, looking for blood and money. Mine! According to *The New York Times*,

> *Polley was named during Senate-investigation hearings in 1971 as an intermediary between unnamed crime figures and a New York Supreme Court judge. Most of Polley's American clients said they were already suspicious of their manager by this point, and the publicity of the hearings convinced several to sever ties with him.*[55]

At the meeting where I could confront him, I could feel the change in his rhythm. His demeanor had altered. He smiled as he always did when he saw us, but he wasn't amused when I asked him, "Where's our $200,000 advance from BMI?" He tried dancing around it by changing the subject. I was singing a different tune, one he hadn't heard before and he didn't know the steps of the dance. He was falling behind the beat. He shifted uneasily in his chair, picking harder than ever at his shiny, ivory polished fingernails. I asked him, "When are we going to receive the documents from the copyright of-

[55] IBID.

fice to confirm our ownership of "Yellow Ribbon?" It was time to take off the gloves.

Irwin and I spent the next two month in the office of our attorney Peter Parcher, preparing for our trial against Polley. I listened attentively, while Irwin daydreamed. "You take care of this, Brown", he would say. "You're good at this shit".

On the last day of the trial, Irwin was called as a witness. He vainly tried to pull open the gate leading to the witness box. He kept pulling on it. The jurors watched, some snickering until the bailiff showed him that it opened by simply pushing it inward. He was doing his Laurel and Hardy routine without even trying. Peter Parcher, who would one day go on to establish himself as one of the premier litigators in the history of our business, leaned over to me and whispered, "We just won!"

> Parcher has repeatedly rescued a rogues' gallery of trouble-prone or troublesome stars: The Rolling Stones, Bob Dylan, Bruce Springsteen and Paul Simon, as well as boxer-thug Mike Tyson, author Frank McCourt, the estate of Andy War-

> hol and titans such as Sony and Time Warner...
> When singer Luther Vandross was charged with
> manslaughter after his best friend died in a car
> accident with Vandross driving ... Parcher de-
> vised a decidedly slick defense: An olive tree had
> dropped its slippery nuggets precisely where the
> crash occurred on Laurel Canyon Boulevard. "It
> might as well have been ice and snow", Vandross
> walked... Parcher likens his courtroom style to
> his training in Tai Chi, a martial arts discipline
> that his instructor describes as "steel wrapped in
> velvet". Made up of equal parts of Clarence Dar-
> row, Sam Spade and Swifty Lazar, he is known
> for a doggedness that a rival lawyer once likened
> to "trying to pull a Rottweiler off your [private
> parts]".[56]

Peter didn't know how right he was. While the jury was out the news reached everyone that Peter Ham, the lead singer of the rock band, Badfinger, (another unwitting member of Polley's stable of 'cash cows') had committed suicide, implicating Stanley as the 'soulless bastard' who stole his money. We were probably the two most successful songwriters at that point and time in the industry and look at what he was trying to do to us.

It's a great lesson, if you want to be in this business

---

[56] Steel Wrapped in Velvet, When Bruce Springsteen, Bob Dylan or the Rolling Stones have a date in court, they call on Peter Parcher, by Robert Lenzner. Forbes Magazine, http://www.forbes.com/forbes/2001/0430/092.html

be aware of where your money is and remember that anyone you hire is after a percentage of your pie. Listen carefully to the slick promises and remember that some of your representation "team" may try to steal the whole pie. Listen to me, learn enough of the business to not get screwed all of the time.

> In 1972, Polley negotiated a record contract with Warner Bros. Records for Badfinger, which called for advances to be paid into an escrow account. In 1974, Warner's publishing division filed a lawsuit against Polley when it was unsuccessful in locating the funds. The legal morass crippled Badfinger financially; bandleader Pete Ham committed suicide in 1975 leaving behind a note pointing the finger at Polley for his financial ruin.[57]

And,

> In Al Kooper's memoir Backstage Passes and Backstabbing Bastards, Kooper squarely pins the blame for Ham and Evans' suicides on the band's manager, Stanley Polley. Al Kooper also worked under Polley and had this to say about him: "Polley reminded me of Dr. [Hannibal] Lechter from the Thomas Harris books. An acknowledged brilliant doctor, but one who just happened to eat a few of his patients".[58]

---
57 Stanly Polley, biography, The World Public Library, http://netlibrary.net/Article.aspx?ArticleId=0002576839&Title=Stan%20Polley.
58 Without You by Bad Finger. Songfests, http://www.songfacts.com/detail.php?id=17779.

Irwin and I prevailed. We were now publishers of our own songs. We were the captains of our ship and our houses were in order. We followed "Yellow Ribbon" with three consecutive hits for Tony Orlando, "Who's in the Strawberry Patch with Sally", "Steppin' Out Gonna' Boogie Tonight" and in the style of Irwin's favorite blast from the past, Al Jolson "Say Has Anybody Seen My Sweet Gypsy Rose"?[59]

That was the last hit I wrote with Irwin Jesse Levine. In three short years, we had killed them, mowed them down. We were America's hottest song writing team and as innocently as it had begun, that's how it ended. We were done.

---

59 Tony Orlando and Dawn recorded "Say, Has Anybody Seen My Sweet Gypsy Rose" written by Irwin Levine and L. Russell Brown, (1974) Bell Records

We were very happy
Well at least I thought we were
Can't somebody tell me
What's got into her
A house, a home, a family
And a man who loves her so
Who'd believe she'd leave us
To join a burlesque show?
Say has anybody seen my
Sweet Gypsy Rose?
Here's her picture when she was my
Sweet Mary Jo
Now she's got rings on her fingers
And bells on her toes
Say has anybody seen my
Sweet Gypsy Rose?
Oh, I got wind my Jo's been dancin'
Here in New Orleans
In this smoke-filled honky-tonk
They call the land of dreams
Now, here she comes a-struttin'
In her birthday clothes
Say has anybody seen my
Sweet Gypsy Rose?
Baby, baby
Won't cha come home
We all miss ya
And every night we kiss your picture

Rose, one night the lights go dim
And the crowd goes home
That's the day you wake up
And you'll find you're all alone
So let's say goodbye to Gypsy
Hello Mary Jo
Say has anybody seen my
Sweet Gypsy Rose?
(Instrumental)
So take those rings off your fingers
And bells off your toes
Say has anybody seen my
Now you know just what I mean by
Has anybody seen my Sweet Gypsy Rose?

Chapter 18

Schmoozing with the Legends

The term "schmoozing" is defined in the industry as hanging with the industry's stars, executives, and creative superstars. The fame of "Yellow Ribbon" opened many doors to me except the one at Studio 54, the famous and outrageous nightclub in New York City. It was lit up like a Christmas tree every night, but it was a dark place. It was the ultimate fantasy home-away-from-home for rich thrill seekers.

They came from Long Island and the New Jersey suburbs. They were the models, Broadway show dancers and actors who every night mingled with movie stars and politicians. The sexual revolution was in full swing. We were now officially out of control. Massage parlors were springing up all over town. The perennial 'happy ending' was the topic of conversation at every power lunch meeting. "Fairy tales" were coming true.

I had a love-hate feeling for the place, for the muscle-bound bouncers out front who let in only the 'beautiful' people (beautiful in the eyes of Steve Rubell, the 'ring master' flying two inches off the floor, the guy who had created the circus), to the wild anticipation I felt when I was finally admitted. I wanted to see what the heck all the excitement was about.

> *Regarded as master promoters, Mr. Rubell and his longtime partner, Ian Schrager, 42, were hailed at the height of the disco craze in the late 1970's as the "first pashas of disco." Owning and operating the enormously popular nightclub on West 54th Street that opened in April 1977 and is now defunct, they hosted celebrities and society figures and their bevies of hangers-on, selectively admitting customers at the door.*[60]

I had tried unsuccessfully several times to be admitted to Studio 54, wearing a two-foot high Indian feather taped to my forehead and some gigantic white-framed sunglasses. This time my long flowing gown was the clincher, as I walked down the long seedy corridor that

---

[60] Steve Rubell, Studio 54's Creator And a 'Pasha of Disco,' Dies at 45, by Peter B. Flint. New York Times, Obituaries, http://www.nytimes.com/1989/07/27/obituaries/steve-rubell-studio-54-s-creator-and-a-pasha-of-disco-dies-at-45.html

led to the most exciting dance floor in the history of the world. It was a safe haven for gays, drug users, and hard-core sex addicts.

I had to dress the part to get admitted. It was the place to be if you were anybody. And you were a nobody if you weren't on the "A" list of people who were ushered in through the velvet ropes strung up around the entrance. It was the living, breathing, culmination of the rebellion that found its voice in the 60s and was now screaming, "I'm coming out!"

The Fifth Season, a brothel right out of the pages of Sodom and Gomorrah, was also a favorite haunt for the rich and famous. Members had a special code they typed into a keypad, hidden under a blue canopy, positioned outside the front door. Awaiting them were gorgeous, nude young girls (some were professional strippers) parading in front of a swimming pool filled with multi colored balloons. Someone must have missed a protection payment and eventually it was closed down (just in time to avoid the Aids epidemic that was right around the corner).

The rock n' roll music I knew and loved was losing ground. The strains of country music and R&B that were so ingrained in me were also being drowned out by the 'four on the floor' insane-incessant dance beat of 'disco' music!

I used my Club 54 experience and the "sound" I'd heard there to create a new sound. Dance music ruled the day. Radio stations all over the world were jumping on the bandwagon and I knew I would be left in the wake if I didn't get on board. The great artists of the sixties, who had monopolized *Billboard's HOT 100* list, overnight were becoming yesterday's news, like me. But not for long!

One night, while I was home with the kids, I finally got to see the movie, *Star Wars*. We were enthralled, locked in to the story. But when Luke and Obie Wan were at the 'way' station, trying to hitch a ride to Oberon, I heard that weird intergalactic band of musicians playing that strange sounding song. I tuned out of the story and into the music.

Lisa had a song title she had given me days before and with her writing the lyric, and that 'alien' *Star Wars*' band providing the kick in the ass I needed for inspiration, I wrote my first disco hit "Gone, Gone, Gone". I booked two of the greatest guitar players of the day, David Spinoza and Jay Berliner, along with Paul Griffin, everyone's 'go-to-guy' on keyboards. Charlie Conrad, my engineer and the owner of The House of Music recording studio, turned me on to an insane drummer, the infamous Bernard "Pretty" Purdie. With the amazing Will Lee on bass, I took a page out of the Bob Crewe's 'How to Make a Hit Record' handbook.

I had the nucleus of the band I needed to cut a great demo. I pitched the song to Jack Gold, Johnny Mathis's producer. Hank not only put Mathis on my tracks, he paid me for my demo which become the hit single. Jack got Gene Page, a brilliant arranger, to add wizard like string parts to my demo and the results ended up on the BBC top ten charts for 6 months.

Lisa and I always liked to fly to Antigua in the Caribbean, for songwriting inspiration. Something about the waves coming in seems to clear my mind in a way that stirs my songwriting creativity. Once, while there on business, Lisa ran into a young lady from England. They got into a conversation about their lives and when Lisa mentioned that she'd co-written "Gone, Gone, Gone", the woman was so thankful (she loved the song), she asked Lisa if she could hold her hand. It was gratifying to Lisa to see how much fans are touched by the power of great songs and the artists who record them.

Like me, Bob Crewe was not a schooled musician. I had learned by watching him in action and boy, was he ever in-action at a recording session. The most important ingredient when making a record is the ability to communicate. Those out-of-the-box ideas of his had become mine. Ideas like "I want a waterfall here, a bright colored sound, a sexy rhythm, make it blue!"

Dancing, pleading, cajoling, whatever it takes to get the point across to the musicians and arrangers who grew accustomed to this special quality for making a record. I adopted it. You can still hear Elvis breathing on his guitar track. You can hear the orchestra bleeding on Sinatra's vocal mike. It's the imperfection that often makes recordings "perfect".

Lisa told me about a great singer she had heard about from her friends. We went to see him at the local Holiday Inn, near our house in North Caldwell. He lived up to his billing. He was a dynamic blue-eyed soul singer, a New York guy, a street guy, named Billy Vera. We bonded immediately. We wrote together and I landed him a record contract with Bob Reno's Midland International record company.

At the Hit Factory recording studio in the heart of New York City, I was putting the finishing touches on Billy's album. I went out for a break and in between Studios (A) and (B) there was a wooden church style chair that sat only two people. I was sitting there, clearing my head, when this guy bounds out of Studio (A) and squeezes in next to me. I turned and looked John Lennon (1940-1980), dead in the eye.

I blurted out, "I'm L. Russell Brown. I wrote, "Tie A Yellow Ribbon Round the Ole Oak Tree", and I love you". Without missing a beat, he grabbed me in a headlock and feigned punching me in the head while ranting, "That bloody song never stops playing". "It's driving me fucking crazy and you wrote it?" All I could say was "I copied it from you, John!" Lennon smiled, looked at me with that devilish grin of his and said, "Amateurs copy Brown, we steal".

For some strange reason, President Nixon had expressed in the media his dislike of Lennon. He said 'Trick Dicky' was trying to have him thrown out of the country. John said, "The Kennedys' are trying to help me, but I need all the help I can get. Can you help?" I shrugged, "I don't know, John, but I'll try if you want me to".

He asked me to follow him into Studio A. He wanted my opinion on a new song he was recording. The studio was jam packed with forty or more violin players sawing away on his song, "I'm Scared". He turned to me and asked in that distinct, Liverpool accent (that had been so instrumental in transforming four unknown boys into the world's most famous quartet), "What do you think, Brown?" Lennon asking me for my opinion! What do 'I' think, he wanted to know? "Are you nuts, John?" "What do I think?" "I can't even breathe!" We shook hands. He smiled and said goodbye and I went back to my Billy Vera session across the hall in Studio B. Sadly, one day we all heard the news about Lennon. It was awful of course, but for someone like me who met and talked to him, it was heartbreaking.

> *Former Beatle John Lennon, the 40-year-old . . . the most popular rock group in history, was shot to death. . . as he stepped from a limousine outside his home in the Dakota, an exclusive apartment building on Central Park West and 72nd St. Police arrested a suspect, "described as a local screwball", minutes after the shooting and charged him with Lennon's murder. The "smirking" suspect, identified as Mark David Chapman, 25, of Hawaii, was seen in the vicinity of the Dakota for several hours before the shooting and reportedly had hounded Lennon for an autograph several times in the last three or four days.*[61]

---

[61] John Lennon Death Anniversary: Legendary Beatles singer shot dead by Mark David Chapman (Originally published by the Daily News on Dec. 09, 1980. This story was written by

Had I been more of an opportunist, which I have so often failed to be, who knows, I may have gotten in touch with him? We may have become friends. Even written a song together. Imagine, if we could have been writing a song together that horrible, fateful day in December.

Years later, while walking across 58th Street and 7th Avenue, I happened to pass a young man holding hands with an elderly woman. I felt a shiver down my spine. I knew it was him, Paul McCartney! The very last thing a personality in the industry like myself should be is an animated fan of the famous and powerful in the industry when meeting or schmoozing.

Never ask for a photograph, selfie, or autograph period. However, I must be honest, I really do enjoy meeting people who have changed the world and letting them know how much I appreciate their creative efforts. I know that success in this business is tied to courage, talent, luck, the ability to thrive on rejection, passion, and most importantly, damn hard work. I reached the curb

---
Patrick Doyle, Robert Lane and Hugh Bracken.) The New York Daily News, http://www.nydailynews.com/new-york/john-lennon-killed-mark-chapman-month-1980-article-1.2035505

and waited. I couldn't contain myself. As he stepped on the curb next to me, I reached out my hand and said, all in one breath, "I'm L. Russell Brown and I wrote 'Tie a Yellow Ribbon Round the Ole Oak Tree'." "I think you're the Mozart (1756-1791) of our time and it's a thrill to shake your hand".

McCartney gave me a puzzled look, turned and began walking north, towards Central Park. After a few steps, he turned around, looked at me and said, "I don't know about the 'Mozart of our time' thing, but it's a thrill to shake your hand". He was larger than life. I felt like I was a fifteen-year old kid again in the first row at the Brooklyn Paramount Theatre. My insides were screaming. I was a star struck fan again. I love Paul McCartney, period.

On one of our countless flights to Los Angeles, Lisa and I were sitting several seats away from one of the greatest movie icons of all time Mr. *Citizen Kane* and *War of The Worlds* genius, the great Orson Welles (1915-1985). She insisted I say hello to him. I told her no way. It was common knowledge that the man coveted his privacy and it will surely upset him if a complete stranger approaches him. Lisa sternly said, "If you don't do it, I will!"

I reluctantly got up, walked over to the two seats this enormous hulk of a man was sitting in, looked down into his piercing eyes and somehow got it out "Hi, I'm L. Russell Brown and I wrote, 'Tie A Yellow Ribbon Round the Ole Oak Tree'." Welles lit up like a Christmas tree, reached out and grabbed me, put me on his lap, kissed me on the cheek and said, "That's my favorite song!" And with that he pushed me back up, slapped me on my ass and told me to go back to my seat. I smiled at him, he smiled back. I went back to my seat to tell Lisa, "Thanks, honey, you were right".

It's the imperfection of perfection, like the un-tuned vocal of the incomparable Johnny Mathis on our song, "Gone, Gone, Gone" that led me to meeting John Belushi. Mathis' recording of that song of mine rocked my world and brought it and me back to life in 1979!

My first thought after finishing the demo was, "Who owes me a favor?" Jack Gold (1921-1992), an in-house producer for *Columbia Records*, did who was one of the execs who had turned down "Yellow Ribbon". I once had an opportunity to remind him of it and embarrass him in front of his boss but instead I said, "I should have shown that song to you first, Jack". At that, Jack whispered in my ear, "Thank you, Larry, bring me another song, I'll record it, guaranteed".

I called him and told him about "Gone, Gone, Gone". He was cutting a new Johnny Mathis album and told me to jump on a plane and come out to LA. The first-class ticket I bought provided me with more privileges than I had anticipated. I took a window seat on the right side of the plane. I glanced over to the other side of the aisle and spotted a man wearing a lumberjack jacket and construction work boots. He was already dozing off with his face pressed against the window. It was John Belushi (1949-1982).

I wanted to say hello and waited for the opportunity.

He got up to have a Merritt at the front of the plane. Back in those days you were still allowed to smoke on airplanes. I followed him, "I'm L. Russell Brown" and after giving him my usual "yada-yada-yada", he shoved his hand into my shoulder and said, "What Yellow Ribbon? I never heard of no "Yellow Ribbon".

He motioned to a stewardess to come over to us asking her, "Did you ever hear of, 'Tie A Yellow Ribbon Round the Ole Oak Tree'?" Before she could answer, he burst out laughing, asking me, "Didn't you ever see 'The Best of Belushi'? I play Beethoven creating "Yellow Ribbon!" It's a scream, one of my best bits".

Realizing that I had been had, like so many of his lovable victims on *Saturday Night Live*, I was thrilled. We sat and talked for hours, which went by like minutes. I felt I knew him all my life. He was the coolest dude. The real McCoy, what you saw was what you got from John Belushi. Near the end of the flight he implored me to stay at his hotel, The Chateau Marmont. He would 'see to it' that I got a room. I rode with him in his limo back to the hotel. We checked in, said goodnight, and the next day I went to the Johnny Mathis recording session.

I walked into the control room. Jack was listening to Mathis sing, "Gone, Gone, Gone", and my insides began to fall out. I turned to Jack and told him, "He's got to sing it more soulful, Jack". Jack agreed but he wasn't going to tell him, so he said, "You go out there and tell him yourself, Larry". Johnny Mathis, one of the greatest recording artists in the history of music was recording my song and I wanted it to be perfect! But I didn't care who he was, it wasn't good enough for me. I hadn't yet heard the great Will Roger's quote, "I never miss a good chance to shut up", so I went out into the studio and asked Mathis, "Could you sing it a little 'blacker?"

With that, Mathis glared at me and put me in my proverbial place. "I think I got a handle on this, why don't you go back inside the control room?" He had gotten the message. His next take rocked me and was a sensation in the UK and Europe that year.

I returned to the hotel and dialed Belushi's room 629. I remembered his room number because it was the same number as my birthday, June 29. He said, "Hello' and I answered, "Hello, John?" To my amazement he said, "Is that you, Larry?" I told him I was booked to leave on a 7:00 pm flight. He invited me up to his room to watch a Cincinnati football game on TV. "You got plenty of time. Bring me two of your pillows, you're not gonna' need them". I put on a black golf glove and held the two pillows in my left hand. When he answered the door, I grabbed his face with my gloved hand and he gasped, "You're f--cking crazy, Brown" as he laughed and ushered me in.

He had lox and bagels in the room and we ate, but that wasn't all he had on his plate (drugs). I couldn't cut it anymore, not even for him-not one line. He fell asleep clutching his electric guitar. It was time for me to go. I picked up the guitar and played and sang the chorus to "Yellow Ribbon" segueing into "Lullaby, and

Goodnight!" I put down the guitar and leaned over and kissed him goodbye on his forehead. He smiled up at me. How could I have known it would be the last time I would ever see this beautiful human being, one of my favorite people in the world. How I hate cocaine! John Belushi died in the same room, number 629, not a 'happy birthday to me'.

> *John Belushi was born in Chicago . . . to Agnes Demetrio (Samaras) and Adam Belushi, a restaurant owner. Through a young hellion in grade school, John became the perfect all American boy during his high school years where he was co-captain of the Wheaton Central High School football team and was elected homecoming king his senior year. He also developed and interest in acting and appeared in the high school variety show. He helped found the "West Compass Player" . . . An improv comedy troupe patterned after Chicago's famous "Second City" ensemble. While working on Saturday Night Live he appeared in the movie Goin' South . . . which led to him being cast in National Lampoon's Animal House . . . and other movies. In 1982 while working on another screen play (called 'Dry Rot'), he checked into the Chateau Marmot celebrity hotel in Los Angeles. On March 5, Belushi was found dead in his hotel room at the age of 33.[62]*

I was invited by my nemesis, the great composer Char-

---

62 John Belushi, biography.IMDb, http://www.imdb.com/name/nm0000004/bio

lie Fox (the man who won the Grammy for song of the year with "Killing Me Softly") to close his annual, "Songs of Our Lives" show in Hollywood, California.

> *It was estimated at one time that the music of prolific composer/producer Charles Fox was heard by 300 million people each week as the composer, along with frequent collaborator, lyricist Norman Gimbel, of the themes of such '70s hit TV shows as Happy Days, "Our Dreams Come True" from Laverne and Shirley, Angie, The Love Boat, Wonder Woman, Love American Style, and Paper Chase.*[63]

Our granddaughter was 15 years old and she accompanied Lisa and me to the festivities. She had never seen me perform before. She sat with Lisa in the third row and I sang every song to her. She was wearing a silver heart that Lisa had bought for her on Rodeo Drive, and I never saw her look more radiant as she looked staring up at me standing there, seeing only her adorable face. I was inspired. Charlie gave me a glowing introduction. I stood at the mike for several seconds and said nothing.

I looked off stage where Charlie was standing and said,

---
[63] Charles Fox, Biography by Ed Hogan. allmusic.com, http://www.allmusic.com/artist/charles-fox-mn0000805450/biography

"You know folks in 1974, along with my dearly departed friend and writing partner Irwin Levine, I was nominated for the Grammy for Song of the Year". "Needless to say, Charlie and his songwriting cohort Norman Gimble won". "Ever since that day, I've wanted to get my hands around Charlie's neck and choke him".

I heard gasps from the audience (at this remark), as the stage was set. "But tonight, for honoring me with the privilege of closing this show, for this most worthy cause, supported by you such wonderful people, I want to put my hands around Charlie's neck and hug him".

Charlie was beaming and we've been pals ever since. On my way, back to the Beverly Wilshire Hotel, I got a call from Lisa. The girls needed shampoo, how could I say no. Larry King made me happy that I didn't. I met him as I was leaving the Rite-Aid drugstore. He was checking his prescriptions when I looked at him and said (as he stared at me with oh no, another pest), "I'm L. Russell Brown and I wrote 'Tie a Yellow Ribbon Round the Ole Oak Tree'." With that, he exclaimed,

"Wow! that's one of my favorite songs, it's a classic." We walked and talked for several blocks. I liked him, as he was just the nicest guy. What you see is what you get. There's only one Larry King.

"Yellow Ribbon" was still inspiring others in ways I could never have imagined. A very brave lady, Penelope (Penne) Laingen started a national movement to use yellow ribbons tied around trees to protest the Iranian hostages and the lack of President Carter and the State Department to bring them back home.

Bruce Laingen, former Ambassador to Malta and Penne's husband, was then serving in Teheran as the Charge d'Affaires just a few months before the U.S. Embassy was overrun by student protesters. According to a US diplomatic history source,

> "At the hour of attack, Charge d'Affaires Bruce Laingen, Deputy Chief of Mission Victor Thomseth and Security Officer Mike Howland were at the Foreign Ministry, where they became "semi-hostages" until captured by the militants and put into solitary confinement in a prison near the end of the crisis".[64]

[64] "An Online Exploration of Diplomatic History and Foreign Affairs." A Brief History of U.S. Diplomacy. Accessed June 24, 2017. http://www.usdiplomacy.org/history/service/brucelaingen.php.

The student take-over of the embassy and the threats to kill all of the American hostages become the lead story on the nightly news. Penne was frustrated and just didn't know what to do. The *Washington Post* published stories about the crisis as the hostage crisis wore on. Author Barbara Parker wrote about the American public's "IRage" and made Penne Laingen's story about waiting for her husband's release part of the dialog.[65]

Out of frustration, Mrs. Laingen made a great suggestion while being interviewed by the national media. She said, "Tell them to do something constructive, because we need a great deal of patience. Just tell them to tie a yellow ribbon around the old oak tree".[66] The comment hit a "national" theme that united the public. Irwin and I once again became celebrity's over-night. The press came knocking on our doors. We were interviewed. I was overwhelmed, honored, proud to be an American.

---

65 Parsons, Gerald E. "How the Yellow Ribbon Became a National Folk Symbol." How the Yellow Ribbon Became a National Folk Symbol (The American Folklife Center, Library of Congress). 1991. Accessed June 24, 2017. https://www.loc.gov/folklife/ribbons/ribbons.html.
66 Association for Diplomatic Studies and Training Foreign Affairs Oral History Program Foreign Service Spouse Series, Penelope Laingen. Interviewed by: Jewell Fenzi Initial interview date: March 27, 1986. http://www.adst.org/OH%20TOCs/Laingen,%20Penelope.toc.pdf

Before long, hundreds of thousands of people-millions, were tying ribbons around trees, placing them on their doors and displaying them on the bumpers of their cars and trucks. During the Gulf War the tradition widened. American flags were adorned with yellow ribbons. Our song had created an American Tradition. When a child was reported missing, yellow ribbons were displayed as a symbol of hope for their safe return.

England adopted the tradition. I remember seeing several news stories from the BBC using yellow ribbons to signify the safe return of British citizens. The craze spread across the Pacific to the Far East and back home. It appears that it has even inspired support of people waging the war against cancer, support groups colored their ribbons pink.

I am humbled and grateful for how many people have wanted to show me their appreciation for writing the song. One night I received a phone call from the public relations department at Camp Pendleton, the Marine base just north of San Diego. They requested I make an appearance at a dedication ceremony and asked if I would bring a few signed copies of the sheet music to "Tie A Yellow Ribbon". When I arrived at the main gate I was directed to the Ranch, a sprawling house that was General James T. Conway's residence.

> *General James T. Conway served as the 34th Commandant of the United States Marine Corps. As Commandant, General Conway served as the senior uniformed Marine responsible for the organization, training, and equipping of over 250,000 active duty, reserve, and civilian personnel throughout the United States and overseas, as well as the management of the $40 billion annual Marine Corps budget. Prior to becoming the Commandant, General Conway served for four years on the Joint Chiefs of Staff as J-3, or senior operations officer in the U.S. military, where he oversaw the war efforts in Iraq and Afghanistan. As a member of the Joint Chiefs of Staff, General Conway functioned as a military advisor to the Secretary of Defense, the National Security Council, and the President.*[67]

I pulled up to a group of Marines directing traffic. "It looks like something really important is happening here". "I don't want to be in the way, where should I park?" The young NCO asked me, "Are you L. Russell

---

[67] General James Conway, U.S. Marine Corps (Ret.) 34TH COMMANDANT, UNITED STATES MARINE CORPS (CO-CHAIR). Securing America's Future Energy. http://www.secureenergy.org/energy-security-leadership-council/general-james-conway-us-marine-corps-ret

Brown?" "Uh, yeah, why?" He responded, "We've been waiting for you". At that moment a score of Marines, in full regalia with medals displayed on their chests (that spoke volumes about who they were and where they had been), gathered around me in the parking lot. The highest-ranking officer in attendance asked me, "How does it feel to have written a song that helped unify our nation?"

I got out of my car and began shaking hands with some pretty impressive young leathernecks. Handing out signed copies of sheet music, I answered, "All I gave is a song, you guys gave your blood". I was escorted to the Ranch and was introduced to the General's wife. She told me that he was in Baghdad, commanding his troops, but he "wished he could have been here to meet you".

The 'Gunny' and I hit it off like we were long lost friends. He gave me a tour of the Ranch that ended as we entered a very interesting room. I noticed a lone couch and to the right, resting on a lectern, was an open guest book. Photos of past Presidents, sitting on that very same couch, adorned the walls.

The 'Gunny' with a friendly push said, "Sit down, I'm gonna' take your picture". I said, "I'm not big enough to sit in this chair". He laughed, took my picture, and told me. "It's going on the wall". He handed me a pen and asked me if I would sign the guest book "Under the last signature". I hesitated, then signed my name directly under President George W. Bush!

Tony Orlando and Dawn had landed their own weekly television show and overnight Tony became a household word. His personality beamed on television. He was a natural showman. He became a superstar. Everyone who was anyone wanted to be on his show. While at the Grammys, Irwin and I had a confrontation with Tony over business that resulted in our estrangement from him, which lasted over twenty-five years. He never mentioned our names on his TV show. We never stood next to him and sang together. That is, not until after Irwin died, when I called him. During that call, we repaired the wounds and have become grateful for one another's friendship.

Tony Orlando invited me to Branson, Missouri to be a part of his annual Veteran's Day tribute. I pulled into the parking lot and was escorted to a special parking area. As the guard opened the gate, he pointed to a sign that read, 'RESERVED TONY ORLANDO' and told me to park there. Tony was waiting for me in his dressing room. We reminisced for a while and then he left to go on stage. I was again escorted (this time to sit in the same row as the Medal of Honor winners).

> *The Medal of Honor is the highest award for valor in action against an enemy force, which can be bestowed upon an individual serving in the Armed Services of the United States. Generally presented to its recipient by the President of the United States of America in the name of Congress.*[68]

During the show, Tony walked off the stage and up the aisle towards our seats. He asked the Medal of Honor winners to stand up. The crowd roared. He then asked those heroes if they knew who they were sitting next

---
68 The Medal of Honor, The Medal of Honor Society. http://www.cmohs.org/society-history.php

to and proceeded to say, "This is my 'mortgage payment', my 'shoes', the 'shirt on my back'. The man who wrote, 'Tie A Yellow Ribbon Round the Ole Oak Tree'."

The audience rose out of their seats as Tony lifted me out of mine, put the microphone up to my face and asked, "How does it feel to have written a song that helped bring our nation together?" I took the microphone from him. With my arm around Tony, I turned to the audience, and said, "Tony's got it wrong folks, this amazing man is "my 'mortgage payment', my 'shoes' and the 'clothes on my back".

With tears in his eyes and in mine too he pulled me up to the stage with him and announced to the crowd, "This is my George M. Cohan". We sang "Yankee Doodle Dandy". We danced together. We then argued about who was going to start "Gypsy Rose". He insisted, "You start, Larry". I sang the first half of the intro and he sang the second half. We belted out the rest of the song together and brought the house down.

I want to believe that if Irwin were still alive, time would have healed the wounds for him too. He would have been on that stage with Tony and me celebrating our lives together. It was Irwin who insisted we never speak to Tony again.

I came to realize I owed a big part of my life to Tony Orlando! And I couldn't wait to tell him that. Now, Tony is my dear friend and the voice of my greatest songs. Songs are like flowers. No matter how beautiful and sweet, unless they are promptly delivered, they wilt and die. TONY ORLANDO has been delivering my songs flawlessly, non-stop, since he turned them into classics. Without his spectacular talents, there would most probably be no L. Russell Brown. God Bless Him!

Chapter 19

It Took a Long Time

Like most people who never had any money Lisa and I wanted to see what it could buy. We bought everything. Everything we always dreamed of. Everything that we were so sure would bring us more happiness, new clothes, new cars, and a big new home, with a beautiful Olympic sized swimming pool. I bought a new habit too, the expensive deadly habit of drugs.

Things deteriorated quickly. I was out of control. We began fighting and the verbal abuse turned ugly. We had started out like the Beverly Hillbillies and were fast becoming the Hatfields and McCoys of North Caldwell, New Jersey. But we still loved each other and knew we had to get away to save our marriage. We flew to Antigua with the girls and following yet another argument, Lisa told me she couldn't take anymore. We needed a miracle and none in sight.

Or, so we thought. She left me and wandered aimlessly down the beach, with our little girls in tow, trying to figure out what in the world she was going to do. Out of the blue stepped a man in a bathing suit, a middle aged, affable looking, balding Irishman. Walking along the beach with his older brother, he stopped and began a conversation with Lisa. Carrying my guitar, I caught up to them and she introduced me to John Ryan and his brother, Frank.

I immediately liked him. I felt that somehow this was a kindred spirit. I wanted to get to know him better although I didn't know why. We decided to have a talk together after dinner. We met on the top of the mountain overlooking Dickinson Bay, one of Antigua's most beautiful stretches of beach, in a restaurant known back then as, Clouds. After dinner, Lisa and the girls went back to our room. I went outside to a small sitting area where John Ryan was waiting for me.

He asked me about my guitar playing and if I was ever

in a band. In typical Larry Brown fashion, I thought I would impress him and ran off a list of my credits. He was fascinated and seemed genuinely interested in hearing my story. I said, "Ryan, I'm pretty good at figuring out what people do for a living". He said, "Oh, yeah, Brown. He paused and looked at me with a glowing, knowing smile that I would soon come to love.

"Let's see if you can figure out what I do". I had gotten his Irish up. Confident, I named one profession after another as he shook his head, gleefully pronouncing, "Nope!" I told him, "I got it, you're a teacher". He responded, "You're getting close, but unfortunately still wrong, Mr. Brown". After a few more feeble attempts I said, "I give up" and met Father John Ryan.

"I've got the parish up in Kinnelon, New Jersey, Larry". I sat back and studied him for a moment. He was wearing black pants and a short-sleeved shirt. Earlier, when I had first met him on the beach, he was wearing a bathing suit. Just a typical tourist. How could I have known? "You're a priest?" He smiled and nodded

"Yes, I'm a priest".

I began to apologize for the profanity I had been using. He cut me off, "Hey, want me to take you around back and teach you some words you haven't heard yet?" He was a regular guy, just like me. We talked for over an hour and discovered that we were both avid golfers. He invited me to play a round at his country club at Rockaway River. I promised to call him.

In the 1950s, most Irish families considered it the highest honor to have a son become a priest. The chapel on the grounds of the Roman Catholic Church, Our Lady of The Magnificat, was built in 1952. This small, unassuming house of God was Father John Ryan's first assigned church. At his first Sunday Mass, he greeted thirty odd people at the entrance. As they filed out they were surprised that he remembered each one of them by name. He had many gifts and so much more that he was about to share with me.

> *In 1961, Bishop McNulty began the Mission Parish in Kinnelon. He appointed Rev. John R. Ryan, a curate at St. Paul's Church in Clifton as*

Administrator of Our Lady of the Magnificat. Fr. Ryan, although born in Morris County, had no idea where Kinnelon was located. He offered the first Mass in the Mission Chapel on Sept. 8th with his brother, Fr. Leo Ryan attending. One year later, Bishop McNulty announced the canonical erection of the Parish of Our Lady of the Magnificat and named Ryan the first Pastor... In 1981, Rev. John Ryan was made a Domestic Prelate by His Holiness, Pope John Paul II with the title of Monsignor.[69]

Life was becoming much more difficult for Lisa and me. I was getting progressively worse. I didn't know if I was going to survive and didn't know if I cared too. I was numb, lifeless. Lisa was on the verge of throwing in the towel. In desperation, I found Father John's number and called him. He said he had been waiting to hear from me as he quickly invited me to come and play a round of golf with him at his country club. I will never forget that day.

By the time, he and I had finished fourteen holes we had talked about everything from religion to great songs. I had a thousand questions. He had two thousand answers. I made him aware of my father's Jewish

---
69 Our Lady of the Magnificat Parish, Parish History, http://olmchurch.org/parishhistory.php.

heritage and my mother's mixed heritage as well. I had been Bar Mitzvah'd but was ambivalent about religion. Still, I was a proud Jew and accepted my faith without reservation.

Father Ryan proved to be an adept golfer. He was beating me soundly and not letting up, not giving an inch. We reached the fifteenth tee. It was a par three, about one hundred sixty-five yards long. He was about to hit his tee shot when I ribbed him, "Padre, you make a hole in one here and I'll convert to Catholicism". John smiled and stood over the ball. He missed hit it-a terrible slice that sailed up towards the outer branches of a tree striking it hard only to land inches from the hole! "We're tryin' son, we're tryin'!"

He kept on trying. He never let up. After revealing that he was a recovering alcoholic, he took me to AA meetings that he was presiding over. He showed me that I was not alone and with his guidance I found the way out. Things began to improve. My hopes were rekindled. Something 'good' had entered my life and something 'bad' was gone.

Eventually, he baptized me. I converted to Catholicism, once I realized that before I met Father Ryan, I was blind to faith, life, living, and to Jesus Christ. While I will never reject my Jewish beliefs, the message Father Ryan provided came directly from God. I was thunderstruck that day at Rockaway River and have been about my beliefs and Father Ryan ever since. Lisa said that fateful day, "No miracle is gonna' happen out here in the middle of nowhere, on this lonely beach".

Was she ever wrong! God had sent us one of his special angels. A man who was loved by more people than any human being I have ever known, until I met Father Joseph Breen years later in Nashville, another one of God's angels. Father John presided over my second marriage to my dear wife Lisa as we renewed our vows.

I knew that I could never repay this Irish Angel for all he had done for my family but I gave him something I had previously refused to give to the Smithsonian Institute. I had been keeping the yellow legal paper Irwin and I had written the original lyrics to "Tie a Yellow Ribbon 'Round the Ole Oak Tree" on. I framed them and inserted a small card with the inscription, "To Father John Ryan, I am giving this to you so that it may be closer to its true creator".

A few months after one of the greatest men I had ever known passed away, his younger brother Leo, a fellow priest, sent me a box containing personal effects of Father John's he had found while cleaning out his brother's house. I opened the box and found the framed original paper with the lyrics to "Yellow Ribbon", along with the card I had put in the frame. Tears well up in my eyes as I write this, but they are tears of joy. At least I had him for a while.

After Father John Ryan died, I couldn't find a spiritual advisor I could relate to as Fr. Ryan was one in a million. I was blessed once again when I met Fr. Joseph Breen. We were at a party where he had a collar on, but I thought he was just a minister. As soon as I looked into his eyes and asked him where he was serving, I knew I had met my new spiritual advisor. We stepped outside where it was cold and dreary and he introduced himself, "Hi, I am Fr. Joseph Breen".

I thought, now here's a guy I can relate to, a rebel, just like me. He has his own website, where he is in favor of almost everything the Vatican was against at one time, but he is loved by the people at the hospice center, Mary Queen of Angels, where he is assigned. The last time I dropped him off after having lunch, a bunch of the residents greeted him warmly. He introduced me as his friend who wrote, "Tie a Yellow Ribbon". Without even thinking about it, I sang, *"I'm comin' home, I've done my time. Now I've got to know what is and isn't mine. If you received my letter telling you I'd soon be free, now you know just how much Fr. Joe Pat means to me!"*

My feelings from my childhood of grief, sadness, loneliness, and anger vanished. I was finely at home in my heart and soul. My life has been a roller coaster ride filled with incredible ups and downs. "It Took a Long

Time to Find This Place", a song I wrote with Bob Crewe and Raymond Bloodworth recorded by Patti La Belle, says it best.[70]

---

[70] Patti LaBelle recorded "It Took a Long Time", written by Bob Crewe, Raymond Bloodworth, and L. Russell Brown, (1974). Epic Records

It took long time to find this place

It took long time to see happy

It took long time to recognize your face

It took long time running around

It took long time for to find this place

It took long time to see happy

It took long time to recognize your face

It took long time running around

Nothing good come easy

Nothing makes it fast

No one ever made love

Overnight too last

So it took so many, many years to meet

'Til we came together

I was incomplete

Yes I was

Took a long time

Took a long time……

Took a long time……

Took a long time……

It took long time to find this place

It took long time to see happy

It took long time to recognize your face

It took long time running around

You're the place of worship

You're the place I stay

Where ever thou will goest

I will go your way

It took long time to find this place

It took long time to see happy

It took long time to recognize your face

It took long time running around

And the rest is history!

Praise the Lord, my soul; all my inmost being, praise his holy name. Praise the Lord, my soul, and forget not all his benefits—who forgives all your sins and heals all your diseases, who redeems your life from the pit and crowns you with love and compassion, who satisfies your desires with good things so that your youth is renewed like the eagles. The Lord works righteousness and justice for all the oppressed.

Psalm 103[71]

---

[71] "Psalm." In The Bible, 612. Nashville, TN: Holman Rainbow Study Bible, 2015.

Authors

L. RUSSELL BROWN

I remember meeting L. Russell Brown for the very first time as I was filling up my Porsche Boxster with cheap gas at a local Costco. He wandered by to compliment my taste in cars. Laughing, I offered to let him take it for a spin, to which he replied "he'd probably kill himself" and his wife would never forgive him. L., as I know him, is one of the nicest guys I've ever met.

He pushed out his hand and introduced himself quickly saying, "Hi, I'm L. Russell Brown and I wrote 'Tie a Yellow Ribbon Round the Ole Oak Tree'. Shaking his hand, I introduced myself saying, "Hi, I'm Dr. Larry Wacholtz, A Professor of Entertainment and Music Business at Belmont University and my kids' great-grandfather wrote 'Silver Bells', 'Mona Lisa', and about a thousand other great hits". We starting laughing as I could see his eyes light up and he yelled "Jay Livingston, one of the greatest writers ever!" "Yeah, and I teach about the music business at Belmont, have a ton of students, some of whom are now in the industry, some very famous. I did psychographic research for MCA Records, and we probably know a bunch of the same people". More laughter!

It's not unusual for me to meet famous people, but meeting L. was like meeting the Energizer Bunny without the pink suit. L. was in his shameless self-promotion mode (just like every other songwriter I know), as he asked me to listen to some of his latest songs. Yes, he's got the white flowing hair and the wrinkles of life's experiences pressed onto his face, just like me, except mine are not as deep.

But listening to him talk about his songs is like hearing a teenage kid talk about his first love after his first date. "Here's one George Strait just recorded for MCA Records, and here's one I'm trying to get to Garth (Brooks)". "Well L.", I responded, "his wife,

Trisha Yearwood, is one of my former students, and, you know that song you just played before that one is something I could probably get to Vince Gill, as I know both Vince and Amy. Not great friends, but we know each other". More laughter.

A few days later L. called and asked to meet for breakfast which, of course, in this town means grits, biscuits, eggs, and probably some gravy thrown in on something. We laughed through the meal and then L. told me why he wanted to connect. Once again, he was into his shameless self-promotion bit, this time about some new songs he'd written for a Broadway play. *The Sunset Gang* was written by Warren Adler, who had also written *War of the Roses, Random Hearts,* and other books, that have been turned into great Hollywood movies.

So, in the parking lot (after breakfast) with the air blasting in his car, L. sang me the entire stage play's musical score. Breathtaking, and a little stunning to see his eyes light up, as he gave me his personal performance. Talk about fun, I was loving it! Then, he said, "Let's get this play stood up (which means to get it into production)". Hasn't happened yet, but it will, that just takes time and lots of green paper.

About a month later, he sent me some notes a friend of his (iconic songwriter Sandy Linzer) had typed into his computer as L. conveyed his life story to him. Over the last couple of years, I've heard those stories many times as he'd bring each to life (usually over lunch), as if he was lifting the type of the pages by breathing life into them.

As you read, consider what L. Russell Brown has accomplished, as a broken child, seriously beaten by an abusive father, living in a housing project as a kid, Jewish, and how (as a kid) he had to steal food for himself, and his brothers, and sisters. His is the story of a good kid in a terrible childhood who seemed far more likely to end up with a large number printed on the back of his shirt, serving time in a state prison.

Instead, he took the narrow path, on a difficult road, and has lived a life of struggle and fame, by following his passion of writing songs that have been recorded by many of the world's greatest superstars. They have made millions of dollars, and at the same time, have touched our hearts, minds, and souls. L.'s songs have given our nation courage in times of desperation and helped us to share our sense of forgiveness. "Tie a Yellow Ribbon Round the Ole Oak Tree" became a symbol for families of hostages, soldiers, and loved ones who were heartfully missed. "Yellow Ribbons" led to the pink ribbons used for cancer awareness, and to other meaningful ways of expressing our shared human grief and sorrows.

Few of us will ever inspire as a deep passion and love for our country, (and for all who serve in uniform) as L.'s songs have. But as you read you'll discover other life events that were also used in his songs including,

- "Knock Three Times" and "Has Anybody Seen My Sweet Gypsy Rose", both recorded by Tony Orlando & Dawn,

- "Bon Bon Vie", the R&B hit by T.S. Monk,

- "C'mon Marianne" sung by Frankie Valli and the Four Seasons, and also in the stage play *Jersey Boys*,

- "I Woke Up in Love This Morning" and "Am I losing You?" performed by The Partridge Family on tour and on their network TV show,

- "I thought I heard my Heart Sing" by country superstar George Strait,

- "Sock it to Me, Baby!" by Mitch Ryder & The Detroit Wheels,

- "Paradise" recorded by Phoebe Cates and used in the movie with the same title,

- "Gone, Gone, Gone" by Johnny Mathis,

- "4 to 1 in Atlanta" by Tracy Byrd,

- "You've Got Me", recorded by the soul lady herself, Etta James,

- "Stop and Think" by Kiki Dee, and

- "It Took a Long Time" by Patti LaBelle.

One of the crazy and endearing things about people who have created life changing entertainment products (songwriters, artists, producers, and label executives) is they don't have a clue about how much their creative efforts have positively changed humanity and global societies.

People are people and songs and great recordings speak to the hearts and minds of all of us. Politics, types of governments, borders, and all that "other" stuff is irrelevant. I remember talking to Jay (Livingston) at his home in California when he was feeling the pains of his age and was quite honestly not very well. He looked me in the eyes and said, "I really don't know if I did anything very important in my life". I still remember my surprise and quick response, "Are you kidding!" "Look at all the joy people feel from all the songs you've written, including every Christmas when 'Silver Bells' is played all the time, everywhere!"

Jay and L. Russell Brown are brothers in spirit when it comes to God-given songwriting talents. Listening to them, they almost seem naïve in their understanding and acceptance of how much their songwriting and creativity have accomplished in bringing joy to humanity. And L. is not finished as he has, since the start of 2017, composed over 70 songs with rock star Dan Auerbach of the super group *The Black Keys*. L. also has songwriting credits on Korean K-pop recording artist Psy's latest release, "I LUV IT", with over 60 million hits on social media.

Life's not easy, even for the most talented of us. Yet for a guy like L., who had a double whammy in front of him, his life is one of inspiration. In today's world, many complain, feel victimized, and demand others notice them. Let's be inspired by his determination to accomplish the impossible. That's a great lesson for all us to remember whenever we think we can't win or accomplish what we really want out of life. His lesson is to believe in God, ourselves, and to take a shot at whatever we want to do with the freedoms offered in our country.

L.'s life is one of a humble New Jersey wise guy, who

had a choice between anger, loneliness, and evil, or a life in the music business where most fail. He used his belief in a higher power and his life's experiences to write from his heart instead of out of anger. His accomplishments might seem more like a piece of fiction, but his is a real story of courage and unthinkable success. At the same time, we are the lucky ones every time we hear one of his songs. He and I, since that day at the gas pump at Costco, have become best friends, and honestly, I am honored to know and share his story with you.

* * * *

Sandy Linzer

Iconic songwriter Sandy Linzer worked with the famous *Bob Crewe* in the early years of rock & roll writing songs for recording artists The Four Seasons, whose hits included "Dawn", "A Lover's Concerto", "Working My Way Back to You", and "Let's Hang On". His songs and recordings have touched millions of fans over the last 50 years as he continues to write songs for, and sometimes produce, superstars including *Kool & the Gang, The Backstreet Boys, Dr. Buzzard's Original Savannah Band, The Toys,* the late *Whitney Houston, N'Sync, Barry Manilow, T.S. Monk, Odyssey, The Spinners, Al Hirt,* and many others.

In addition, Linzer has written soundtracks for movies and network TV shows including *Jersey Boys, Ten Things I Hate About You, Donnie Brasco, The Preacher's Wife, Cheech & Chong's Next Movie* and (you guessed it), many more.

* * * *

Larry Wacholtz PhD.

Dr. Larry Wacholtz is a full professor at the Mike Curb College of Entertainment & Music Business at Belmont University in Nashville Tennessee. As a consultant to industry professionals, his research company Entertainment Media Research (EMR) provided psychographic image research for MCA and Word record recording artists.

Thanks to the Coleman Foundation, Larry was the Director of the original Music Business Entrepreneurship Center at Belmont University. It provided many seminars and workshops for industry wannabes to meet and discuss their business ideas with highly successful industry artists and executives.

Larry developed the first national educational program for recording studios and curriculum for high school students in Memphis TN. He served on the National Academy of Recording Arts and Sciences Board (NARAS Memphis) and has voting rights for the Grammy Awards.

He has authored fifteen books, three movie scripts, and co-written one novel. Dr. Wacholtz was interviewed on two national TV shows in the 1990's discussing his research on consumer preferences tied to various types of songs. He was also the co-producer of the 1974 World's Fair Rock Concert TV show. Most of his works are about how the music and entertainment businesses work and as a college professor he's been published in journals and presented many research papers at entertainment and academic conferences.

Index

Symbols

"4 to 1 in Atlanta" 276–283

A

"Abba Dabba Dabba" 26
Abe 74
Alan Freed 55–296
Alexanderplatz 104–296
Al Jolson 52–296, 183–296, 223–296
American Bandstand 58–296, 163–296, 164–296
American Graffiti 64
"Am I losing You?" 276–296
An Affair to Remember 124
Annette 75
Arc de Triomphe 107–296, 124–296, 125–296
Artist and Repertoire 199–296
ASCAP 158–296
"At the Hop" 65
Aunt Virginia 123

B

Badfinger 217–296, 221–296, 222–296
Ballantine Brewing 27
Barry Mann 137–296
Belmont 272
Belmont University 271–296, 280–296, 281–296
Berlin Wall 101–296, 104–296
Beth Israel 137
"Big Girl's Don't Cry" 178
Billboard's HOT 100 230
Bill Haley and the Comets 56–296
Bing Crosby 17–296, 41–296, 52–296, 170–296
Bloodworth 93–296, 94–296, 102–296, 103–296, 117–296, 137–296, 138–296, 151–296, 154–296, 163–296, 164–296, 165–296, 168–296, 173–296, 266–296
BMI 62–296, 158–296, 159–296, 210–296, 219–296

285

Bobby Hebb 56-296, 167-296, 174-296
Bobby Robinson 66-296, 68-296
Bobby Vee 153
Bob Crewe 15-296, 110-296, 155-296, 156-296, 159-296, 162-296, 231-296, 232-296, 266-296, 279-296
Bob Halley 155-296
"Bon Bon Vie" 276-296
Booker T. and the MGS 56-296
Boys Town 38
Brandenburg Gate 105
Bremerhaven, Germany 120
Brenda Lee 56-296
Brown 4-296, 5-296, 12-296, 23-296, 26-296, 33-296, 37-296, 44-296, 45-296, 46-296, 47-296, 51-296, 74-296, 89-296, 90-296, 91-296, 100-296, 102-296, 110-296, 112-296, 114-296, 115-296, 117-296, 118-296, 131-296, 135-296, 141-296, 142-296, 145-296, 159-296, 165-296, 171-296, 173-296, 174-296, 187-296, 189-296, 190-296, 192-296, 198-296, 199-296, 205-296, 206-296, 208-296, 209-296, 220-296, 223-296, 234-296, 235-296, 237-296, 238-296, 240-296, 242-296, 245-296, 250-296, 259-296, 266-296, 271-296, 274-296, 277-296
Brownie 118-296, 125-296, 126-296, 131-296
Bruce Laingen 246

C

Carmen 107-296, 111-296, 112-296, 118-296, 123-296, 124-296, 125-296, 127-296, 128-296, 129-296, 141-296
Carole King 137
Carole Lombard 53
Champs Elysees 105-296
Charlie Calello 13-296, 206-296
Charlie Conrad 231
Charlie Fox 210-296, 243-296
Chips Moman 187
Chris Dreja 174
Chuck Berry 54-296, 91-296
Cleveland family 25
"C'mon Marianne" 175-296, 176-296, 179-296, 276-296
Cole Porter 54
Columbia Records 52-296, 118-296, 131-296, 192-296, 239, 239-296
Crewe 15-296, 110-296, 155-296, 156-296, 157-296, 159-296, 160-296, 161-296, 162-296, 175-296, 178-296, 191-296, 192-296, 231-296,

232-296, 266-296, 279-296
Cynthia Weil 137

D

Dan Auerbach 13-296, 278-296
David Appell 186-296
David Spinoza 231
Dick Clark 163-296, 164-296, 166-296
Dick Lebo 63
Dick Wegryzn 154-296
Distant Cousins 151-296, 154-296, 163-296, 164-296, 165-296, 173-296, 174-296
Donny Kirshner 137
Doris Day 57
Dotty Tanela 71
Dr. Ingrid Hoffman 146
Dr. McGovern 148
Dwight D. Eisenhower 42
Dynavoice Records 156-296

E

eing caught sneaki 128
Elvis 52-296, 59-296, 61-296, 65-296, 90-296, 91-296, 108-296, 153-296, 187-296, 233-296
Elvis Presley 52-296, 187-296
Epic Records 11-296, 120-296, 266-296
Etta James 276-296
Everly Brother's 151-296, 155-296

F

Father John 259-296, 260-296, 261-296, 263-296, 264-296
Father John Ryan 259-296, 260-296, 264-296
Frankie Valli 15-296, 17-296, 155-296, 156-296, 175-296, 207-296, 276-296
Frankie Valli and the Four Seasons 276-296
Frank Sinatra 14-296, 15-296, 16-296, 27-296, 54-296, 207-296
Frehlinghuysen Avenue 32
Fr. Joseph Breen 264-296, 265-296
Ft. Dix 87-296, 94-296
Ft. Gordon 92-296

Ft. Hood 87-296, 88-296, 91-296

G

Garth (Brooks) 272
Gary Collins 103
Gaudio 175-296, 177-296, 178-296, 179-296
Gene Page 231-296
Gene Pitney 153
General James T. Conway 249
General Louis 102
Gene Vincent 56
George Burns 14-296, 16-296
George Strait 272-296
Gerry Goffin 137
Goldie Hawn 110
"Gone, Gone, Gone" 131-296, 239-296, 241-296, 276-296
Goodfellas 22
Grammy 200-296, 209-296, 210-296, 211-296, 244-296, 245-296
Greenwich Village 151-296
Guillermo "William" B. Williams 54-296

H

Hal Webman 152-296
Hank Medress 185-296, 201-296, 202-296
Happy Days 65
Harlem 68
Harriet 155
Harry James 28-296, 49-296
"Has Anybody Seen My Sweet Gypsy Rose" 275-296
Heidi 145-296, 146-296, 147-296
Here to Eternity 18
Highway 29 77
Hit Factory 233-296

I

im McCarty, 174
Irwin Levine 135-296, 181-296, 183-296, 184-296, 190-296, 192-296, 205-296, 206-296, 223-296, 245-296
"I thought I heard my Heart Sing" 276-283
"It Took a Long Time" 276-296
"I Woke Up in Love This Morning" 192-296, 276-296

288

J

Jack Gold 231-296, 239-296
Jake Mohawk 29-296, 30-296, 31-296, 73-296
Jay Berliner 231
Jeff Beck 165-296, 166-296, 173-296, 174-296
Jennifer 147-296, 148-296, 149-296
Jenny the Tiger 148-296
Jerry Lewis 27-296, 182-296
Jersey Boys 15-296, 175-296, 177-296, 276-296, 280-296
Jimmy Page 165-296, 174-296
Joel Diamond 118-296
John Belushi 238-296, 239-296, 240-296, 243-296
John Lennon 182-296, 233-296, 235-296
Johnny Mathis 131-296, 231-296, 238-296, 239-296, 241-296, 276-296
Johnny Price 139
John Tully 44-296, 63-296

K

Kaddish 47-296
Keith Relf 174
Kiki Dee 276-296
"Knock Three Times" 275-296
Korean K-pop 278

L

Laingen 246-296, 247-296
Landolphi 48-296
Larry Brown 159
Larry King 245
Larry Wacholtz 271-296
Laugh In 110
LaVerne 140-296, 141-296
Lawrence Brown 37
Lesley Gore 162
Lindemann 37
Lisa 4-296, 131-296, 137-296, 139-296, 140-296, 141-296, 143-296,
    144-296, 145-296, 146-296, 160-296, 181-296, 207-296, 209-296,
    211-296, 218-296, 231-296, 232-296, 233-296, 237-296, 238-296,
    244-296, 245-296, 257-296, 258-296, 261-296, 263-296, 271-296
Little Richard 54-296, 61-296, 62-296, 217-296

Longy Zwillman 31–296
L. Russell Brown 271, 271–296
Luther Dixon 183

M

Madge Lewis 72–296
Major Rink 114–296, 115–296
Martin Scorsese 22
MCA 281
MCA Records 272, 272–296
Mike Curb 280–296
Mitch Rider and the Detroit Wheels 110–296
Mitch Ryder & The Detroit Wheels 276–296
'Mona Lisa' 271
Mr. Fitzpatrick 40–296, 41–296
Mr. Lewis 73–296, 74–296, 75–296, 76–296
Mr. Rowe 38–296, 39–296, 115–296
Mr. Rubell 228
Mr. Shaffer 44–296, 46–296
Mr. Talbot 46–296
Murray The K 59–296
Muscle Shoals 187

N

Nancy Sinatra 13
Natalie Wood 14–296, 15–296, 16–296
Nevel 152–296, 153–296, 154–296, 156–296, 157–296
Nevel Nader 152–296, 157–296
Newark 13–296, 18–296, 26–296, 27–296, 29–296, 30–296, 32–296, 37–296, 42–296, 43–296, 47–296, 63–296, 64–296, 76–296, 82–296, 87–296, 88–296, 92–296, 98–296, 115–296, 123–296, 128–296, 140–296, 141–296, 144–296, 207–296, 208–296, 219–296
New Jersey 17–296, 26–296, 28–296, 31–296, 53–296, 56–296, 64–296, 77–296, 87–296, 94–296, 152–296, 182–296, 187–296, 207–296, 227–296, 257–296, 259–296, 278–296

O

ommy Dorsey TV show 59
One Hit Wonder Club 168
or some answ 132

Orson Welles 237–296
Our Lady of The Magnificat 260
Oxman 63–296

P

"Paradise" 118–296, 120–296, 276–296
Paradise 118–296, 119–296, 120–296, 276–296
Paris 94–296, 97–296, 98–296, 99–296, 101–296, 102–296, 105–296,
 107–296, 111–296, 112–296, 118–296, 124–296, 125–296, 133–296
Pat Boone 57
Patti LaBelle 266–296, 276–296
Paul Abbatemarco 142
Paul Griffin 231
Paul McCartney 236–296, 237–296
Paul "Pinky" Brown 25–296
Penelope (Penne) Laingen 246–296
Peter Ham 221
Peter Parcher, 220–296, 221–296
Philip Roth 27
Phillipsburg 77–296
Phil Spector 182–296
Phoebe Cates 118–296, 276–296
Pigalle 97–296, 99–296, 100–296, 105–296, 107–296, 108–296
Psalm 103 268
Psy's 13–296, 278–296

R

Raymond 93–296, 117–296, 154–296, 155–296, 165–296, 174–296, 266–296
Raymond Bloodworth 93–296, 117–296, 165–296, 266–296
R&B music 54–296, 56–296
Reader's Digest 47–296
Rebel Without a Cause 64
RIAA 192–296
Ringo Starr 199
Robert DeNiro 22
Robert Wagner 14
Rock n' Roll Hall of Fame 55–296, 165–296
Rolling Stones 56–296, 62–296, 217–296, 220–296, 221–296
"Roll Over Beethoven" 91–296
Rosemary Clooney 52–296
Roston 145–296

Route 22 77
Russ Columbo 53–296

S

Sammy Cahn 54
Sammy Davis Jr 52
Sam the Sham 166–296, 167–296
Sandy Linzer 4–296, 5–296, 11–296, 274–296, 279–296
Screen Gems Music 137–296
"Sea Cruise" 90
Sergeant Ryder 111–296, 113–296, 114–296, 115–296, 116–296, 117–296
Sergeant Solario 89–296
SESAC 158–296
Seth Boyden 17–296, 23–296, 43–296, 114–296, 187–296
Seth Boyden Housing Projects 23–296
SHAPE 97–296
"She Ain't Lovin You No More" 164–296, 165–296
"Sherry" 178
'Silver Bells' 271
Sinatra 13–296, 14–296, 15–296, 16–296, 17–296, 18–296, 27–296, 28–296, 54–296, 171–296, 207–296, 233–296
"Sock it to Me, Baby!" 276–296
South Side High School 48–296
Spencer Tracy 38
"Spooky Rock" 63
Stanley Polley 191–296, 215–296, 216–296, 222–296
Stan Polley 191–296, 206–296
State Home for Boys 37–296, 41–296, 48–296, 63–296, 81–296, 87–296
State Home for Boys at Jamesburg 37–296, 81–296
St. Jude's 148–296
"Stop and Think" 276–296
Studio 54 227
Syd Goldstein 64–296
Syd's 35–296, 64–296

T

"Teddy Boy" 108–296
Terrence Harvey Junior 215
Thea Zavin 158–296
The Beatles 62–296, 152–296
The Bingville Bugle 52

The Black Keys 278–296
"The Bug Outs" 102–296
The Catman 56
"The Duals" 66–296
The Family 22
The Partridge Family 191–296, 192–296, 276–296
The Righteous Brothers 56–296
The Shawshank Redemption 100–296
The Stupidos 135–296
The Weed 30–296, 33–296, 49–296, 72–296, 74–296, 75–296, 77–296,
    84–296, 85–296, 88–296
'Tie a Yellow Ribbon Round the Ole Oak Tree'. 271–296
Toni Wine 187
Tony Orlando 135–296, 186–296, 190–296, 192–296, 202–296, 205–296,
    223–296, 251–296, 252–296, 254–296, 275–296
Tony Orlando & Dawn 275–296
Tracy Byrd 276–296
Trisha Yearwood 273
T.S. Monk 276–296, 280–296
"Twist and Shout" 109

U

Uncle Arty 82–296
Uncle Joe 47–296, 48–296, 59–296, 84–296, 115–296
U.S. Embassy 133–296, 246–296
USO 103–296

V

Vietnam War 93–296, 209–296
Vince Gill 273

W

"Wait Up Baby" 66–296, 67–296, 70–296
Warren Adler 273
Washington Post 247
Weequahic High School 64–296
Wes Farrell 191–296, 192–296
Whitney Houston 28
WKBW 208
WMCA 175

WNEW 54
WNJR 54
Word records 281

Y

Yardbirds 165–296, 166–296, 167–296, 173–296, 174–296
"Yellow Ribbons" 275–296
"You've Got Me" 276–296

Z

Zwillman 31–296

www.ingramcontent.com/pod-product-compliance
Lightning Source LLC
Chambersburg PA
CBHW030050100526
44591CB00008B/90